Institut für Orientalis

Mittelasienwissenschaft Humbol

Université de Lausanne

Svetlana Gorshenina

The Private Collections of Russian Turkestan

in the Second Half of the 19th and Early 20th Century

Klaus Schwarz Verlag
Berlin – 2004

ISBN: 3-87997-624-4
ANOR 15
© 2004 Klaus Schwarz Verlag
   and Svetlana Gorshenina-Rapin

With the financial contributions of
Martin-Luther-Universität Halle-Wittenberg
Humboldt-Universität Berlin
Fondation du 450e Anniversaire de l'Université de Lausanne

Design by Claude Rapin

Contents

Abbreviations
CGA RUz, F., cat., f., p.: Central'nyj Gosudarstvennyj Arkhiv Respubliki Uzbekistan [Central State Archives of the Republic of Uzbekistan], Fond [fund], Opis' [catalogue], Delo [file], list [page].

Transliteration
In the text Russian names have been adapted to the English pronunciation. In the bibliographical references, the titles have been transcribed according to the following system:

а: a — б: b — в: v — г: g — д: d — е: e — ё: jo — ж: zh —
з: z — и: i — й: j — к: k — л: l — м: m — н: n — о: o — п: p
— р: r — с: s — т: t — у: u — ф: f — х: kh — ц: c — ч: ch —
ш: sh — щ: shch — ь: ' — ъ: " — ы: y — э: è — ю: ju — я: ja

To Alexandra and Claude

I owe my gratitude to Mrs. G.A. Pugachenkova (Tashkent) and G. Marias (Paris), Mr. B.A. Litvinsky (Moscow), H.-P. Francfort (Paris), P. Bernard (Paris), F. Grenet (Paris), A. Naymark (New York), E.V. Rtveladze (Tashkent), V.A. Germanov (Tashkent), R. Muradov (Ashkhabad), V.A. Livshits (Saint-Petersburg), G. Lecuyot (Paris), F.T. Hiebert (Philadelphia), P. Ducrey (Lausanne), who have provided me with precise information and sources and have motivated me over the last few years, as well as Mrs. I. Baldauf (Berlin) and Mr. J. Paul (Halle-Wittenberg), who agreed to help realize this study, the publishing house Klaus Schwarz Verlag (Berlin), Mr. H. Barde for the financial contribution of the Fondation du 450e Anniversaire de l'Université de Lausanne, and Mr. S. Stepantsov (Moscow) and Mrs. D. Le Guillou (Halle) for their translation of my text from Russian into English. My thanks also go to the persons and institutions that have helped to reconstruct the iconographical aspect of the private collections: Mrs. Hofstetter and Mr. E.J. Kläy from the History Museum of Bern; Mrs. Ch. Naffah from the Musée du Quai Branly (Paris), Mr. N.A. Utarbekov and E.R. Asanov from the publishing house Media Land (Tashkent), Mr. N. Makhmudov and R. Kajumov from the Reghistan Museum of Samarkand, Mrs. K. Fitz Gibbon and Mr. A. Hale from the Anahita Gallery (Santa Fe, New Mexico, USA), Mr. M. Vaissier (Chemellier, France), M. Florin from the Geographical Society of Paris, F. Guichard (Paris), O. Weber (Lausanne), the staff of the Central State Archives of the Republic of Uzbekistan, the staff of the Archives of the Hermitage and, for their technical help, Mr. T. Ochilov (Samarkand), the staff of Media Land (Tashkent) and Mr. M. Huber (Olizane Editions, Geneva). Lastly I wish to thank C. Rapin (Paris) and my mother A.T. Gorshenina (Tashkent) for their kind help with the correction of the manuscript and their many useful suggestions.

S. G.-R., Lausanne-Paris, May 2003

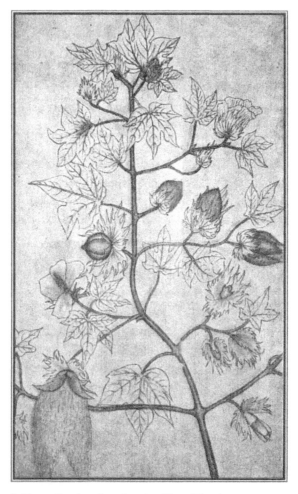

*1. Naturalist drawings in scientific publications:
American cotton cultivated in Russian Turkestan,
end of the 19th century.
Turkestanskij sbornik, t. 527.*

"Studying anticomania *does not imply writing a pamphlet or a satire."*
Annie-France Laurens, Krzysztof Pomian[1]
... Nor preparing to take political steps.

Chapter I

The Traditional Oriental Markets and the Emergence of the Antiques Business in Central Asia

1. Is it Possible to Point out the Characteristic Features of Central Asian Collections?[2]

Although the history of the collections, made in Central Asia[3] in the latter half of the 19th century and in the early 20th century, has not been studied in western literature and has only occasionally been mentioned in Russian and Soviet publications[4], nevertheless, in general, they seem to share the same history as that of European collections[5].

However, although the principles of making and maintaining these collections and their contents, including both *Naturalia* (minerals, plants and animals) and *Artificialia* (ancient and modern works of art and ethnological objects), as well as the intermediate category of drawings of plants or animals[6], have much in common with European collections, Central Asian collections have some rather unique characteristics.

The most important characteristic seems to be the comparatively late spread of the phenomenon of collecting and, consequently, the retrograde development of the antiquarian market (dated the 1840s and 1870s, respectively), as well as the character of the collections, which – unlike European ones – usually do not include

2-4. Naturalist dra-
wings in scientific
publications about
Turkestan, end of
the 19th century.
Turkestanskij
sbornik, t. 527.

works of western art[7], but specialize in local "exotic" objects. These are only of secondary importance in European collections, which tend to give priority to Greek and Roman antiques. On the other hand, after reaching the height of their popularity in the 1880s-1900s, attested indirectly by the growth of periodical publications dedicated to Turkestan collections, antiquarian pursuits in Russian Turkestan gradually began to decline at the beginning of the First World War, which naturally stemmed the flood of tourists in the region, and finally came to an end during the years of the Russian revolution (1917) and civil war. Afterwards, while in Europe *anticomania* had assumed an unprecedented scale by the mid-20th century, in particular, thanks to *la Gazette des Beaux-Arts* founded by Charles Blanc and to Théophile Gautier's activities, on the territory of the Soviet republics antiquarian pursuits went underground. As they were regarded as a kind of semi-legal activity and a manifestation of "hostile bourgeois" morality[8], the collections made before the revolution were nationalized[9].

2. The Advantages and Disadvantages of Being at the "Centre of the World"

The geopolitical situation in the region is largely responsible for its backwardness. For centuries, Central Asia had been located on the highways of intercontinental transit trade, somewhere between the Chinese, the Indian, the Iranian, the Turkic and the Slavonic worlds; this trade flourished in the days of the great ancient and mediaeval empires (the Achaemenids, Alexander and his diadochs, the Kushan dynasty, the Sogdians, the Mongols and the Timurid dynasty); but from the 16th century onwards the region became more and more isolated from the mainstreams of civilization. A combination of several events, different both in terms of their scale and character (the discovery of America by Columbus [1492] and the sea route to India and China by Portuguese sailors [1498][10], innumerable military conflicts between small states and nomads[11], the rise of the Iranian Safavids in the South[12] and the conquest of Kazan [1552] and Astrakhan [1556] by Ivan the Terrible in the North) caused the desolation of the caravan routes of the Great Silk Route and their subsequent re-orientation.

Central Asia lost its status as an important centre of transit trade. Its location at the centre of the Asian continent, which was its trump card during the centuries of its rise to power, was the main reason for its decline, which became more and more apparent[13]. The construction of the Trans-Siberian Railway by the Russians in the late 19th century, left Central Asia well beyond the world trade routes, thus completing the process which had started in the 16th century. On the other hand, geographical and historical information about Transoxiana, having reached its apogee by the end of the Middle Ages – thanks to the accounts of Graeco-Roman[14], Arabic-Persian[15] and European[16] travellers and geographers – was packed with fascinating information, turning Central Asia into a *terra incognita*, one of the world's least studied regions, lying beyond the traditional routes of European travellers'[17]. This is the reason why, up to the 18th century, Central Asian objects are seldom to be found in European collections, in spite of the apparent interest in Europe in all kinds of exotic things (Chinese, Turkic, Indian, American and Egyptian) from the 16th century onwards.

The 16th century marked the beginning of the colonial history of the European powers. The division of the spheres of influence in world geopolitics, which was later to give rise to Russo-British opposition in Central Asia, and put an end to its isolation: from the 18th century onwards the Russians came down to the Amu-Darya at the same time as the British, who came to Northern Afghanistan from India. In this pre-colonial prelude, when rather infrequent expeditions to Central Asia were accompanied by robbers' attacks, plunders, captivation or murders, the tasks of travellers could be far-reaching, including research into geography, geology, biology, zoology, topography, astronomy, history, ethnology, linguistics, and so on. This fact indirectly proves that such expeditions were not so frequent after all and explorers were expected to cover any expenses incurred. Collecting objects, with the exception of objects of natural history, was unusual rather than ordinary[18].

In spite of the great number of Western European (mainly British)[19], and even more numerous Russian expeditions[20] in the 18th century and in the first half of the 19th century, the large-scale discovery of Transoxiana by the outside world began mainly due to Russian expansionism a few decades later[21].

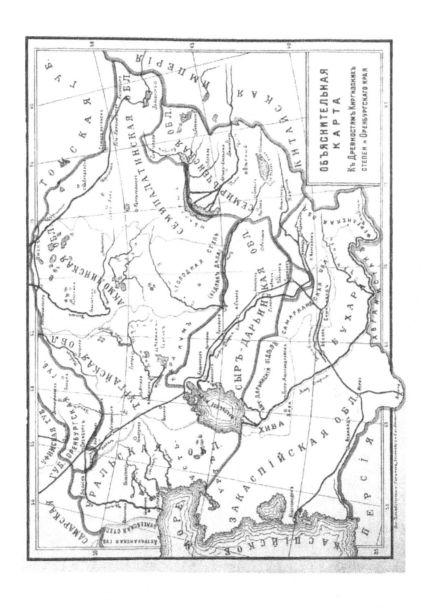

5. Map of Central Asia by J.-A. Castagné, 1910.

3. Russian Colonial Expansionism and the Discovery of Turkestan by the Outside World

Staying within the borders of the Eurasian continent and with no serious natural obstacles to its expansion or sphere of influence, from the 16th century onwards Russia was continually extending its borders, and absorbing neighboring territories, in its search for free access to the oceans of the world.

The landmarks in the first period of Russian expansionism to the south-west, which, at that time, did not come into conflict with any other European colonial power, were: the capture of Azov (1695), the foundation of Orenburg on the border to Central Asia (1735-1737 and 1742), the subjugation of the Black Sea Coast (1774-1795) and a gradual absorption of the Kazakh steppe of the Great, the Middle and the Little Hordes (1731-1846).

The second period, connected with the conquest of Transoxiana, began with the notorious Khivan expedition, undertaken by V.A. Perovsky in 1839, and was marked by an obvious change in motives: the search for free access to the world's oceans, a trade route to India and the desire to enlarge the gold reserves of the tsar's treasury gave rise to the need to reduce British influence in the region, to secure markets for the new Russian bourgeoisie and to meet their demand for raw materials. The internal instability of the Central Asian states, which were ethnically and economically heterogeneous, favoured the realization of these projects.

Two lines of offensive and defensive actions, the Syr-Darya one (1853) and the Siberian one (1854), were united in 1865 to form the border to the Turkestan Region, which was originally under the control of the Orenburg Governor-General. Tashkent was captured in that same year and Samarkand three years later; in 1876 the resistance movement of the Kokand Khanate was also crushed[22].

Politically speaking, military expansion resulted in the establishment of the General Governourship of Turkestan, with the Khanates of Bukhara and Khiva under its protectorate; from an ideological point of view and that of civilization, this led to the incorporation of Central Asia into the Russian and, consequently, the European world and gave rise to the ideas of Moslem reformism, aiming at social modernization (the Djadid movement).

Another consequence of these political events was the development of the collecting of antiques and the establishment of an antiquarian market in Turkestan.

6. Bazaar near to the mosque of Bibi-Khanym in Samarkand, by B.I. Kotovsky, 1932.

4. Traditional Markets of Central Asia

Many pages in the accounts of ancient and mediaeval travellers are dedicated to Central Asian markets, inseparable from the legendary image of the fertile Sogdia and Bactria. The only exception is Anthony Jenkinson who drew the bottom-line by stating, in 1557-1559, that their decay was caused by the diversion of the great trade routes.

Still, in spite of the isolation, by the beginning of the 19th century there were big cities in Turkestan, where local and intercontinental trade was concentrated. In the 1870s the most important city in Transoxiana was Bukhara (70,000 – 75,000 inhabitants), which was also a big trading centre: it had 38 caravanserais, where goods from India, Afghanistan and Iran were stored before being exported further afield[23]. It was closely followed by Tashkent (60,000 –

7. Bazaar in Samarkand, by Barclay, after a photograph, 1880s.

70,000 inhabitants, 18 caravanserais in the central market), which by the end of the tsarist colonial epoch usurped leadership in Central Asian trade because of the severe customs' policy, depriving Bukhara of the benefits of its trade with India[24]. Samarkand and Kokand came next, each having 30,000 inhabitants[25].

However, the existence of rich oriental markets where one could find many ancient and modern things worth collecting (especially for specialized ethnographical collections) did not necessarily imply the existence of a specialized antiquarian market.

Traditional bazaars did not differentiate between ancient and modern objects, because they were not only market-places, but were also the workshops of local handicraftsmen: both were sold in specialized corporative market-rows at comparable prices, without any regard for their antiquity or historical worth. The locals sold ancient coins by their weight to Indian shroffs, and – according to travellers' accounts – it was on these shroffs' stalls that numismatic proto-collections were concentrated. Well-preserved ancient metal and ceramic tableware of local production was used for its original purpose and sold in tableware shops alongside traditional Chinese porcelain, Iranian faience, Russian products (sometimes made in the famous Gardner's and Kuznetsov's factories, but more often by the Gulin Brothers and Gzhel masters, as well as Russian

8. Antiques shop, end of the 19ᵗʰ century. Anonymous photographer.

silver cups). The first specimens of Russian tableware, which appeared on the markets of Bukhara in the 18th century were not able to compete with Chinese production because of the latter's prices (Russian china and faience was still handmade and therefore expensive even in Central Russia) and by virtue of its artistic characteristics, the products of the Chinese masters was more to the liking of the inhabitants of Central Asia[26]. Western European china, which was initially rare, is represented, in archaeology, by one early

9. Porcelain shop, 1871-1872. Anonymous photographer.

specimen of a coffee cup made of Saxonian china dating from the 1760s, discovered on the territory of the ark (citadel) in Bukhara in the 18th century layer[27]. Later, according to A. Vambery, European production, including English china, was quite common on the markets of Bukhara, which were overloaded with Russian goods[28]. According to E. Schuyler, Swiss and English silver watches were cheaper at the bazaar in Tashkent than in Moscow[29].

The situation with regard to carpets, arms, chased copper, manuscripts and lithographed books was very much the same. Archaeological objects were practically absent from the bazaars up to the early 1870s.

10. European society in the chalet of a Bukharan garden, by L. Blot, 1905.

5. The Development of the Antiquarian Market in Russian Turkestan

The situation changed after the mass migration of the Russian population. Thus, the Slavonic population grew from 1.3% of the total number of inhabitants (78,980) in 1870 to 31% in 1914, when the population stood at 271,000. The "New Town" in Tashkent, where the European inhabitants were concentrated, had 2,500 men in 1871, and over 50,000 in 1909[30]. According to data compiled by A. Boutroue (which requires critical analysis), by the end of the 1890s more than

11. Knives merchants, 1871-1872.
Anonymous photographer.

600,000 Russians were living to the east of the Caspian Sea[31]. This increase in the European population was also due to the growing number of western travellers (including those taking part in research expeditions)[32], especially after the construction of the Trans-Caspian railway[33].

After the "dead season" (1780s to 1830s), marked by revolutionary, military and social disturbances, *anticomania* regained its influence in Europe and, at the beginning of the 19th century, had many adherents in Russia (often Baltic Germans). Some decades later it reached Turkestan. Tourists, eager to gain new impressions,

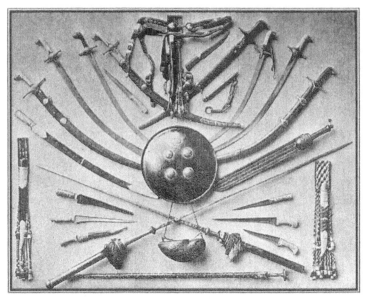

12. Moser's collection of Bukharan arms, 1880s.

found their way to the country, thus provoking a burst of new interest in the "antiques" of the recently conquered Russian colony. This interest was intensified by the beginning of archaeological excavations in Central Asia (Samarkand, 1873)[34], which also made the native inhabitants of Turkestan realize the true value of archaeological objects, and, consequently, of antiques in general.

At this time there was both a demand for "antiques" and a steady supply, and by the late 1880s, a new professional class had come into being – the "antikachi" (dealers in antiques), who, as a rule, did not search for or collect antiques themselves, but bought "antiques" and old things from the local inhabitants.

However, the antiquarian business did not become a specialized kind of trade on the bazaars, where corporative specialization, depending on the nature of the goods sold, remained the main principle. Nevertheless, it underwent certain changes: by the end of the 1880s there was no longer a "row of arms" (which was famous for its Damask steel). New arms were sold on the "iron row" and selling old arms had become the prerogative of the antiquarian traders, usually working "to order". Moreover, by the 1890s expensive

13. Merchants of Bukhara, by Yermakov, 1890s.

goods had begun to be sold on the bazaars "off the hands", i.e. in the open, which had not been common practice before.

In an attempt to satisfy the ever growing needs of private collectors as well as those of the collectors in charge of the big European and Russian museum collections, who sent their emissaries to Central Asia, the Turkestanian antiquarian market gradually became more specialized (the archaeologist V.L. Vyatkin from Samarkand was the first person to mention the high degree of specialization of some individual traders). Antiquarian dealers sprang up in practically all of the big cities, and in Samarkand, according to evidence procured by V.V. Bartold, D.I. Evarnitsky and L.S. Barszscewski, even a sort of "exchange" of antiques was established on the bazaars (1900s)[35]. The traders ("antikachi") used to gather there, fixing the prices and acting as exclusive dealers in transactions involving collectors and suppliers of antiques, who, at that time, were called "archaeological agents". The imperial regulations, according to which all finds of archaeological worth had to be handed over to the state treasury, had no effect whatsoever as local officials would misappropriate the confiscated things or set a minimum price for them, thus – indirectly – encouraging "antiquity seekers" to turn instead to the "antikachi". The same principle worked at a higher level, too. According to G.N. Chabrov, Governor-General K.P. von Kaufmann was offered a catalogue of "curiosities left after the death of the former Sultan of Kuldja, Abil Bay Ibragimov" including the Sultan's sumptuous parade attire, saddle, harness, arms, "steel helmet with golden adornments and plume embroidered with gold and covered with precious stones", stone snuff-boxes, and so on. A special commission had estimated that seven objects, chosen by K.P. von Kaufmann, were worth 1,710 roubles, but K.P. von Kaufmann immediately changed the sum to 750 roubles[36].

14. Caravanserais (Kush-begi), 1871-1872. Anonymous photographer.

At this time Russian and European individuals, travelling or residing in Turkestan, began to prefer to purchase antiques themselves in the towns where there were no antiquarian traders (Karshi, Shahr-i Sabz) or "at the caravanserais at first hand"[37]. Thus, in Shahr-i Sabz, V.V. Krestovsky bought kugmans of "old chasing" and arms, including "a steel shield of old Khorasan work, incised with golden inscriptions"; in Karshi he bought two jars with wash-basins at an "awfully high price" (140 roubles)[38].

By the mid-1900' s, the "antikachi" were ubiquitous in all the cities of Turkestan. In Tashkent antiques were sold by Talib-Khodja Abdulmalikov, his brother and a certain "Sharipka", who traded in

15. Dyeing of fabrics, 1871-1872. Anonymous photographer.

16. Batik printing, 1871-1872. Anonymous photographer.

17. Silk weaving, 1871-1872. Anonymous photographer.

18. Weaving-loom, 1871-1872. Anonymous photographer.

old arms, manuscripts, embroidery, ceramics and coins, supplied by numerous "agents" in towns and villages. In Samarkand, David Junusov and Shakariants sold chased objects and embroidery. In Bukhara there was a well-known trader, David, who often brought things to order directly to the clientele at home and Khodja-Malkhak ("Pilgrim-Angel"). In Khodjent antiques were sold by Mîr Sabir and, in Karshi, by Mullâ Nadjmuddin.

By 1910 the antiquarian trade network, trading with Russia, Europe and America, had reached the height of its development: now things from Central Asia came onto the European antiquarian market which, for example, made it possible for the Swiss collector, H. Moser, to enrich his Turkestan collection by buying things in antique shops in Europe. This situation seems to contrast sharply with that of 1863, when A. Vambery, who found it practically

impossible to take anything from Turkestan, wrote – obviously disappointed: "It was with greatest difficulty that I acquired a very small number of manuscripts in Bukhara and Samarkand; and with a heavy heart I had to leave behind some works which would have filled many gaps in our Oriental Studies"[39].

After the outbreak of W.W.I the legal antiquarian market in Turkestan came to a standstill and disappeared until the beginning of the disintegration of the USSR in the latter half of the 1980s.

19. Weavers, 1871-1872.
Anonymous photographer.

6. Specialization of the Antiques Markets

By the late 1880s and early 1890s a trend towards specialization had already become obvious on the antique markets both in the big traditional trading centres of Bukhara, Samarkand and Kokand and

20. Sale of cotton fabrics, Bukhara, n.d. Anonymous photographer.

21. Sale of cotton fabrics, 1871-1872. Anonymous photographer.

in the new ones, which grew up at the time.

The largest antiquarian market was in Bukhara[40], where, according to the memoirs of the French traveller, A. Boutroue, "the colours are brighter and the mixture of races greater than at the bazaars of Cairo, Constantinople, Tunis or Damascus"[41].

The city of Bukhara, a renowned Central Asian centre of Moslem theology, was especially famous for its "book rows" (*dasta-yi kitab-furushan*), concentrated in the *tim* (market) of Abdullah-khân and on the city bazaar. Here priceless manuscripts were to be seen, including works by Narshakhi and Firdousi, as well as lithographed and later printed books, both of local origin (in Turkestan, book printing began in the early 1880s), and from Kazan, the Crimea, Iran, India and Turkey. The most important bookseller in Bukhara (according to V.L. Vyatkin there were about 25-30 of them) was Mullâ Sheref Al-dîn. Each bookseller offered his visitors about 50 manuscripts and books or sometimes even more. Rare books, though, were never brought to the bazaar or exhibited in shop windows; instead they were stored in the houses or caravanserais and were offered for sale only at the customer's request or at rather high prices[42].

Together with ethnic objects, including the golden embroidery characteristic of this region, archaeological finds (from the sites of Khodji-Abon near Bukhara and Shulljuk-tepe near Karshi[43]) and coins ("Graeco-Bactrian, Arabian, Moslem" and European) were far from uncommon in Bukhara. However, ancients gems of Graeco-Roman, Scythian and Graeco-Indian origin, which were comparatively common on the markets of Turkestan, were not so abundant in Bukhara, despite the fact that there was an old man named Khadja-Malkhak ("Pilgrim-Angel") who was specialized in selling them[44]. The city had many professional sellers of "enamelled tiles"[45] and precious stones from Badakhshan (turquoise, topazes, sapphires and rubies)[46], as well as carpets, as "the carpets' bazaar is one of the most curious to visit; every variety of carpet can be found there, from the simple felt of the nomad to the most magnificent textile"[47]. As regards expensive old carpets the commercial situation was similar to the one of old books.

Samarkand, the Central Asian city best known to Europeans, which for several years from 1888 onwards was the terminus of the

22. Sale of clothes (khalats), 1871-1872. Anonymous photographer.

23. Sale of caps (tjubitejka), 1928. Anonymous photographer.

Trans-Caspian railway (the main 'artery' bringing the would-be buyers from Russia and foreign lands), had a market which was certainly not inferior to that of Bukhara, though the city itself was inferior in the eyes of foreigners: "the city is less interesting than Bukhara, for its local colours have faded because of its contact with the Russians, who have important establishments here and dominate completely"[48].

On the markets of Samarkand there was a wide range of objects typical of Central Asian collections: carpets, both local and brought from the regions corresponding to Turkmenia, Kazakhstan, Eastern Turkestan and India in order to be sold more quickly and at higher prices, traditional embroidery (susani), jewels, metal goods, ceramics from the Samanid period (from the 9th and 10th century) which were extremely popular with collectors, tiles from the famous monuments of the Timurid period (14th-15th century) and archaeological objects supplied regularly by Afrasiab, a big site to the north of the city, known to the ancient Greeks as Marakanda[49].

Kokand was a centre of the carpet trade, specializing in carpets from Kazakhstan and Xinjiang. Besides, there were many manuscripts, miniatures and traditional oriental robes (khalats) here, including Bukharan gold-embroidery robes, Chinese silk and brocade ones. Many travellers paid special attention to the local chasers. According to the evidence of the French traveller, Ch.-E. Ujfalvy, "the local market is undoubtedly the most beautiful and the richest in Russian Turkestan [...] Here one can find everything produced in Central Asia: Bukharan velvet, silk and camel-wool fabric from Marghilan, copper goods from Karshi and Kokand, where the metal workers are extremely skilful, golden and silver works with some turquoise inlays – manufactured with great skill and taste, leather bags from Bukhara, Dungan head-dresses from Western China, Samarkand knives, kaftans made of bright silk, old jewellery, objects made of onyx and jade, hand-made embroidery on fabric and leather, skull-caps (tjubitejka) [...] big embroiderd trunks, cases, and so on..."[50].

According to the studies of Russian Iranist and historian, A.A. Semenov, many antiques were to be found in Karshi, where antiquarian traders appeared somewhat later, despite the fact that it was the second most important centre of the book trade (the bookstall of

24. Jeweller (Zargar), n.d. Anonymous photographer.

25. Samara Scientific Expedition. Carpet and fabrics (adrasse) merchant at Besh-ire, by N. Karazin, 1860s-1870s.

Mullâ Najm Al-dîn was particularly famous)[51].

The main region of the highly specialized carpet trade was the Trans-Caspian Region, Ashkhabad being its centre; here the "Bukharan" (i.e. Uzbek, Afghan and Balochi) carpets prevailed[52]. "Tekinian" (Turkmenian) carpets were concentrated in Merv, and "Kashgarian" (East Turkestani and Indian) could be found on the markets of Samarkand and Kokand[53]. Besides, in the Trans-Caspian district, skull caps, cheap and crude china, leather cases for it and big trunks were sold, which were indispensable to nomads. Archaeological objects were quite common in Ashkhabad. A.A. Semenov wrote: "In the passage running from the Grand Hotel to the central Bazaar Street, Armenian and Lezghin sellers would settle down sometimes right on the brick sidewalk with their cases covered with glass. In these cases one could always see excellent Parthian silver coins, sometimes alongside dark red sard gems. Some of the specimens were very good"[54]. But, as a rule, manuscripts were neither to be found in the Trans-Caspian Region, nor in Semirechye.

Manuscripts were abundant on the bazaars of Ferghana and the nearby district, but not in archaeological and numismatic collections.

Various coins were the speciality of the markets in Kuliab, Kobadian (the ruins of Bishkend, 40 km from the town) and Termez[55], situated along the Afghan borders, where the tradition put the legendary Graeco-Bactrian empire, which even today provides an important part of the numismatic discoveries relating to the Hellenistic and Kushan periods[56].

Tashkent must have been a very attractive place for the "antikachi". The administrative and military élite was concentrated there, as was the White House of the Turkestan Governor-General with its many collections, which began to be compiled as soon as the construction of the governor's residence was finished in 1866. Moreover, here was where the Turkestanian Circle of Friends of Archaeology was founded in 1895, which declared the collecting of antiques to be one of its official aims, as well as several museums and a public library, to say nothing of numerous collectors among the residents of Tashkent (A.I. Dobrosmyslov, A.A. Polovtsev, N.F. Petrovsky, I.T. Poslavsky and others).

26. Potters, 1871-1872. Anonymous photographer.

27. Potters bazaar at Bukhara by Hordet, 1880s.

28. Cabinet-maker, 1871-1872. Anonymous photographer.

29. Merchant of naskadu, 1930-1931. Anonymous photographer.

But, although it was the main town in the region, Tashkent had neither antique stalls in its older parts, nor local antique traders, perhaps because of its high degree of Russification and its tendency to imitate Saint-Petersburg in every possible way. Only in the centre of the city, in Sobornaya Street (Karl Marx Street during the Soviet period, now Sayligokh Street) leading to the White House of the Governor-General were there two shops selling "Asian curiosities" in the 1890s, decorated in a fancy oriental style, one of which belonged to Talib-Khodja Abdulmalikov and his brother[57].

Gems were brought to Tashkent by the "blessed man of Khodjent" Mîr Sabir, who according to A.A. Semenov, was prone to embellish the stories of the acquisition of his antiques and their discovery with fantastic details. They were also brought in by casual people and travellers[58]. Opinions about the bazaar of Tashkent vary according to the periods or the purpose of the travellers. Eventually an antiquarian market grew up here as well, although it remained very unexciting and made no real impression on travellers (cf. Marcel Monnier's words: "The bazaar of Tashkent is very mediocre, far inferior to those of Kokand and Samarkand"[59]). But, the traditional handicrafts charmed H. Moser, who devoted many pages to this bazaar, observing that it constituted a town within a town. According to him, the poorest bazaar was the one in Khiva, which was gloomy and flooded with imported objects from Russia: "there we see only a few finished products, with the exception of *khalats* and *tshugermahs*; therefore it is difficult to collect *bibelots*"[60].

7. Falsification of Antiques

Another characteristic feature of the "specialized" antiquarian markets were the counterfeits of Western European and oriental production, which had flooded them by the second half of the 19th century, but were unknown before then in Turkestan. In 1887 N. I. Veselovsky published a famous paper about counterfeit antiques in Central Asia, denying their presence in the region because of the incapacity of the local artisans to produce them and the general lack of an antiques market[61]. However, he himself had often fallen victim to merchants who sold him counterfeits, which later entered the

30. Counterfeits with mixed Scythian and Graeco-Roman elements.

31. Askos of Termez.

32. Shoe-makers. n.d. Anonymous photographer.

33. Azizbaev's shoes shop in Tashkent, end of the 19th century. Scherer, 1903.

collections of the Hermitage[62]. The Oriental ones include copper works chased in "Iranian style" and Turkish majolica mentioned by V.L. Vyatkin in 1904, as well as copies of ancient ceramic objects produced in contemporary Crimean workshops (Kertch) and counterfeit terracotta figurines (cited by V.V. Bartold). The technology used to produce these figurines was described by V.V. Bartold and E.K. Kverfel'd, who pointed out that terracottas were made in moulds, underwent thermal treatment and were boiled in lard soup, the fissures appearing after that being filled with special powder. V.V. Bartold also mentioned the high price of the fakes at the beginning of an "expert's" activities to one rouble after the over-saturation of the market and their disclosure.

Counterfeit carpets, old arms and embroidery are mentioned by practically everyone who visited Turkestan at this time. Thus, there were plenty of tricks for making carpets look old. In particular, tricksters would use poor quality pigments, wash the carpets many times over, "burn them out" in the sun, or leave them on dusty roads, which numerous caravans passed by[63].

There were also forged coins. Thus, in 1896 the Russian Imperial Archaeological Committee returned to a certain Kakhramon Malik-Muradov a false tetradrachm of Antiochos made by Khodji, a jeweller (zargar) from Samarkand. Among the falsified coins were the "Sasanian drachms" (mentioned by V.L. Vyatkin in 1904) and the coins of Soter Megas whose silver copies ended up later, for instance, in the Moscow Museum of Oriental Cultures and in the American Numismatic Society[64].

Even more curious are the counterfeit "antiques" brought by the European travellers to Turkestan, lost in the middle of Asia where the presence of a Russian official and military élite, interested in collecting antiques, made it possible to sell them at a profit, especially as the remoteness of the region reduced all suspicions.

Among the counterfeits of this kind, which in keeping with the taste of the epoch were influenced by *Egyptomania*, "Egyptian motifs" were not uncommon. In this respect the "richest" collection was that of General A.S. Galkin: terracotta figurines of Egyptian ushabitis, a glazed tile depicting a bull being slain, surrounded by "Egyptian hieroglyphs or imitations of them", and a fibula with hieroglyphs and enamel "Egyptian chariot battle scenes" on it[65].

34. The house in Tashkent of the Swedish merchant Samuel Salm, end of the 19th century. Anonymous photographer.

35. The house of the Governor-General Rostovtsev, n.d. Anonymous photographer.

Hellenistic predilections are seen in another fake: a pseudo-Kushan vase with a moulded relief ("askos of Termez"). Forged in Graeco-Roman style in Naples in the first half of the 19th century after an engraving by Jean-Baptiste Piranese and his son, Francesco, at the workshop of Boccia, and for many years regarded by reputable Soviet scholars as a genuine work, it was part of the collection of I.T. Poslavsky, who bought it from a Termez resident, and later took it to the Museum of the History of Uzbekistan in Tashkent[66].

In the opinion of P. Bernard, this category of counterfeits includes three Roman "finds", preserved in the Hermitage and bought in 1902 by S.M. Dudin in Samarkand from the local "anti-kachi" (two ceramic lamps decorated with scenes depicting Heracles fighting with the hydra, a boar being torn apart by dogs and a ceramic sculpture of a chariot with the three Graces and a nude character sitting in front)[67].

A detailed analysis is perhaps necessary to prove the authenticity of the finds mentioned by M.E. Masson as genuine imported objects, namely to prove the authenticity of the "Egyptian bottle from the collection of B.N. Kastalsky, a scarab-shaped seal made of black haematite with a figure of a man and an antelope turning its back carved upon it, found 2 km downstream from the Charminar bridge over the Dargom at a depth of 1 m and preserved in the Samarkand Historical Museum, and a bronze statuette of a reclining naked man seizing the gorge of the lion attacking him, found at an excavation in Afrasiab by prince Trubetskoy in 1878"[68]. As pointed out by P. Bernard about the Palmyrenian stelae of Merv, the presence of authentic antiques have, like the counterfeits, to be reinterpreted at the light of the probable existence of a real business of antiques independent of the local history[68b].

8. The Decline of Traditional Crafts

Parallel to the growing number of counterfeit antiques was a decline in traditional crafts, unable to withstand the competition from cheap Russian mass-produced goods.

According to the memoirs of two Russian ladies, Olga Lobri and Varvara Dukhovskaya, who visited Turkestan on their journey

to these parts, old carpets had become a rarity on the bazaar of
Tashkent, and old ceramics were fast disappearing from the market
of Samarkand, where as early as 1897 one could not find a single
dish "of old design". The attempt to collect old things in Kokand
for the 1900 World Exhibition in Paris practically failed[69]. In 1907
panic-stricken comments appeared in newspapers, announcing the
end to Turkmenian carpet and wood-carving, such as those things
produced in Azal and Pend, and metal tableware with chased decoration[70]. In 1909 V.D. Pelc, engaged by the Museum of
Anthropology and Ethnography (the Kunstkamera) to buy Sarts'
and Tajiks' traditional clothes reported that the choice in the high
mountain villages had been reduced to a bare minimum: "because
of the poverty of the population and the enormous influx of Russian
products. In the towns, clothes made of traditional fabrics practically did not exist any more"[71]. In 1914 the Russian baron, A.A.
Falkersam (Fal'kerzam), states even more categorically: "No old
things seem to be left on the bazaars"[72].

In the new specialized "Asiatic shops" rare old things were still
to be found, alongside modern ones, but the differences in price
were becoming more noticeable. Prices were going up: Chinese
porcelain was "no cheaper than in Petersburg"[73]. "A visitor cannot
find anything worth buying here", E. Markov said in 1901[74].

Nevertheless, in Tashkent, it was easy to buy all kinds of
modern productions by Ferghana artisans, including modern
Andijan carpets and Kokand silverware for the World Exhibition of
1903 in Saint-Louis[75]. Artisans, who had previously made individual things to order, began to be guided more and more by the market, filling it with mass production articles instead of high quality
works of art (sophisticated but uncomfortable furniture with an
oriental touch – that is a combination of European design and local
ornament – became very popular with Europeans: e.g. upholstered
furniture with embroidered silk "à la susani" was ordered by K.P.
von Kaufmann and A.A. Polovtsev[76]). According to H. Moser, "the
European taste tends to replace […] the beautiful local antique
ornaments. There I see, to my astonishment, tablecloths decorated
with an Etruscan pattern; the salesman is shocked because I let
them in and choose, from his stock, old rags whose colours though
faded are brightened up by their precious oriental pattern"[77].

Chapter II

The Collections:
Formation, Export, Current Location,
Publications

9. Other Ways of Acquiring Objects for Collections besides Buying them

Buying *antiques and modern local artefacts from markets* was the most usual way of collecting in the period in question, and every collector, without exception, resorted to this method. However, there were other ways of acquiring pieces for collections. The following ways are described in order of decreasing importance.

After buying things from markets, the second most popular source of collectable objects were *archaeological excavations* and archaeological material found at ancient sites. This method of collecting was resorted to by almost everyone interested in antiques. Worth noting are the methods used by General A.V. Komarov, who "enriched his collections by making Cossacks, during their expeditions and on patrols, pick up everything on the surface of

36. Excavations of the Ulug Beg's Observatory in Samarkand by V.L. Vyatkin, 1908-1909, by Polyakov (?)

37. V.L. Vyatkin, n.d. Anonymous photographer.

ancient sites after it had rained"[78]. Saint-Petersburg's newspaper
Novosti [News] gave a detailed account of General Komarov's
methods. He used to use the services of an "archaeological agent",
known "among the natives by his nickname, Kizil-Tapan the Gold-
Prospector: after a spell of rain he always picks up many golden
fragments in lucky spots. Once he brought the general a golden ring
with a Syrian garnet. As for coins and carved gems, they are picked
up in great abundance. Once 100 Cossacks picked up about 15, 000
(!) coins and carved gems in two hours in Old Merv"[79].

These methods were not so very different from the practices of
the archaeologist, V.L. Vyatkin (one of the first to excavate
Afrasiab professionally and to write a detailed scholarly mono-
graph on it, which was published in 1926) who, in his spare time,
would take bags and go to Afrasiab with his friends, B.N. Kastalsky
and M.V. Stolyariov, to "hunt for skulls" as they used to joke.

From 1873 onwards, the popularity of archaeological excavations and picking up things at sites grew in proportion to the deve-

38. *General A.S. Galkin, n.d.*
Anonymous photographer.

lopment of archaeological research in this region. It reached its peak in the 1890s and gradually decreased in inverse proportion to the tightening up of Russian legal regulations, prohibiting archaeological research without the special permission of the Russian imperial archaeological committee.

Seizure at war and contributions were only characteristic of the early periods of collecting (in the 1870s) during the annexation of Central Asia. Among the military operations that led to the enrichment of Russian private and state collections, only those shall be pointed out, which are mentioned in documents and publications. This does not apply to General A.S. Galkin's collection: initially sent to suppress Turkmen rebellions of 1916, as a contribution, this general later acquired carpets, gold and silver jewellery, gold and silver oriental coins, as well as precious patrimonial arms. These objects made up his collection, which was later preserved in Semipalatinsk[80].

During the seizure of the palace of the bey of Kitab (1870), a number of manuscripts and archive documents were collected, which – together with other manuscripts obtained during the expedition – were recorded in the register (97 items) kept by the orientalist, A.L. Kun, so that the collection could be handed over to the Public Library in Saint-Petersburg (1871)[81].

On the Khivan expedition in 1873, the orientalist, P.I. Lerch, by order of the Russian Geographical Society, wrote a special instructions booklet on the rules of collecting antiques[82]. This document, together with the hint that valuable manuscripts and archives were

39. The conquest as it has been seen at the Museum of Geok-tepe, 1881.

oft to be found in the possession of qazis and clergy, and a detailed list of the manuscripts much sought after in scholarly circles, explained the rules of preserving manuscripts, the order of a topographical survey of architectural and archaeological monuments, how to copy epigraphic inscriptions and the art of collecting numismatic material. It also recommended making written notes and attaching to them "as many drawings, photographs and plans as possible". The document stated that even partial realization of this programme would "be regarded as an exploit for the sake of scholarship on the part of those who would like to participate in research despite the troubles and difficulties facing their expedition".

On the occasion of this expedition vast collections were made, chiefly by A.L. Kun: manuscripts (partly confiscated from the Khan's palace and taken to the Asiatic Museum in 1874) and documents, including the archives of Khivan khan (transferred to the Saint-Petersburg Public Library[83]). According to the *Turkestanskie Vedomosti* [The Turkestanian News] on 18th December, 1873, he had collected 300 manuscripts. This information was confirmed by the local historiographers of Khiva: for instance, Muhammad Yûsuf Bayânî reiterates this figure when he tells of the manuscripts being taken by Russians from the royal palace[84]. Moreover, Kun's collection[85] comprised 200 stamps "used for minting Khivan khan's coins"[86], 25 of Khivan khan's seals (5 silver and 20 golden ones, mainly belonging to Muhammad Rahîm Khân), Khivan khan's throne, transferred to the Kremlin Armoury[87], 172 Jochid coins, three of Khivan khan's coins from the Kungrad dynasty and ethnographical objects (golden and silver female jewellery, harnesses and arms were transferred to the Tsarskoe Selo Armoury; a Khivan costume, saddles and harness decorated with silver and turquoise were sent to the Dashkova Ethnographic Museum in Moscow; later some of these objects became part of the collections of the Moscow Polytechnical Museum, the Museum of the Society for the Promotion of the Art, and, from 1885, the Hermitage[88]).

Together with his own drawings, Captain D.M. Rezvoi brought from Kunya-Urgench a collection of tiles and household articles. The Central Asian collection of Grand Duke N.K. Romanov was also based on the objects captured during the Khivan expedition of 1873: the lock on the gates to the Khan's palace and an "elegantly moulded" gun from the fortress of Hazarasp, presented to Grand Duke N.K. Romanov and to Prince Eugeny Maksimilianovich by K.P. von Kaufmann to commemorate "the first artillery fire"; a sabre, a saddle, a bridle and a shabrack belonging to the Khan of Khiva and given, in person, to the prince near Urgench, and two caps belonging to the Kazakh Sultan, Kenisara Kasymov[89]. It is worth pointing out the observation of the mining engineer and collector, I.N. Glushkov, who noted that "after the fall of Khiva half of the contributions ordered by General Kaufmann to be made by the Turkmen-Yomuds as a penalty for their anti-Russian actions the women have paid for with their jewellery"[90].

The Kokand expedition of 1875 yielded arms and excellent metal tableware[91], 130 manuscripts and the archives of the

40. Turkmen women, n.d.
Anonymous photographer.

41. General M.G. Chernyaev,
by M.E. van Muyden, 1880s.

Kokand khans[92], transferred to the Public Library in Saint-Petersburg in 1876-1877 (collected by the orientalist A.L. Kun). In addition to this, A.L. Kun took a trip from Kokand to Andijan, bringing back arms and other antiques, which later were offered to the Tsarskoye Selo Armoury[93].

After the capture of Geok-tepe, General N.I. Grodekov came into the possession of "a whole collection of Turkmen manuscripts, found by Russian troops in mosques and medressahs"[94].

The collection of the White House in Tashkent, made possible due to the efforts of all of the governor-generals of Turkestan, was based upon the collection of arms belonging to the Kokand Commandant of Tashkent Mullâ Alim-kul, who died during the assault on the city; at first it constituted part of General M.G. Chernyaev's collection (the collection of precious arms and other objects was later stored in Chernyaev's flat in Saint-Petersburg)[95].

This category includes the collection of 213 manuscripts confiscated in 1898 from Muhammad Ali-Sabirov (Dukchi ishan), which was given to the Turkestanian Circle of Friends of Archaeology in Tashkent and later (from 1900 to 1902) sent, in part, to Saint-Petersburg[96], and some curiosities which entered the collections of foreigners who were witness to Russian offensive operations (Englishman D. Ker, American J.A. MacGahan and German H. Stumm at the assault of Khiva in 1873, Swiss H. Moser at the assault of Samarkand in 1868).

The social background of the people who made up collections, in this way, is confined to participants in military operations.

Presents and gifts, whose richness and luxuriousness were sometimes reminiscent of a disguised bribe, were by no means a common way of enriching collections. They were a form of diplomatic contact rather than a regular method of collecting. A typical example of this was the collection of the Turkestan governor-generals at the White House, consisting partly of the objects offered by the khans of Bukhara and Khiva (arms, ceramics, copper objects, carpets, a big embroidered tablecloth) and exhibited in a parade White sitting-room, painted by local artists from Kokand, in a Little

42. Presents from the Bukharan Emir, by M.E. van Muyden, 1880s.

43. Horse-present of the Khivian Emir to the Pope,
by M.E. van Muyden, 1880s.

44. The Bukharan Emir's Sitorai Mokhi-khosa Palace, n.d.
Anonymous photographer.

sitting-room and Oriental room next to a Winter Garden where "the
decoration of low divans and cushions are a reminder of the buildings of Samarkand"[97]. According to M.E. Masson, among the carpets and the arms which decorated the walls truly valuable objects
were very rare, but it did not worry the governor-generals because
the articles had been valued as luxuries and not as pieces of collections[98].

Among the other examples are Russian Imperial collections.
Between 1876 and 1916 the Emirs of Bukhara and the Khans of
Khiva made some gifts, which after the Revolution of 1917 were
nationalized and transferred to the State Museum of Ethnography in
Saint-Petersburg and the Kunstkamera (expensive oriental robes,
men's belts, susani, handmade silk fabric, parade harness, cold steel
and jewellery). Another is represented by a group of "514 specimens of handmade silk and semi-silk fabric and velvet, presented
to the Russian Tsar by the embassies of the Bukharan Emirs", to be
found in the Museum of Anthropology and Ethnography of the
Russian Academy of Sciences (the Kunstkamera, Saint-Petersburg,
transferred from the State Museum Fund [*Gosudarstvennyj
Muzejnyj Fond*] in the period 1924-1940, collections 2916-2920,
2935, 2936). The Museum of Anthropology and Ethnography also
houses a collection of "arms, offered to the Tsar [during his travels

in Central Asia in 1890-1891] by the Kazakhs of the Akmola Region", susani of Bukhara, parade harness (5,000 items) and transferred there, in 1896 and in 1928, from the Winter Palace[99]. Some other objects belonging to these collections have been transferred to the Asiatic Museum, to the Mineralogical and Zoological Museums[100] and to the Museum of Ethnography in Saint-Petersburg[101].

During the colonial period presents became less and less common, eventually disappearing altogether. Nevertheless, foreign travellers, who regarded a visit to the emirs of Bukhara and Khiva as an essential part of their voyage through Turkestan, still occasional-

45. Types of drawings on silk fabrics (Tashkent, Samarkand, Kokhand, Marghilan, etc.), by Ch.-E. Ujfalvy, 1880s.

46. Bukharan khalat embroidered with gold, 1905-1907.

ly received such presents. H. Moser mentions the gifts received from the Emirs of Bukhara and Khiva, and their administrators in exchange for gifts brought from Russia and Europe. "When I bought the presents, I knew that the manner in which I would be welcomed would be proportional to the richness of my offerings"[102]. The objects received comprised more than 300 dresses [khalats] "in Indian gold cloth,

Kashmir shawls, and silk of a variegated assortment of colours; richly embroidered camel wool turban clothes, enough to delight any European woman; finally, a series of exceptionally large and coloured Persian and Bukharan carpets", "the kind which is not possible to buy, produced for the kings and priceless", several richly harnessed horses, about which a traveller would wonder "if everything was not an illusion", arms, specially a silver dagger-sword, greyhounds, falcons, and a manuscript from the Turkmenian poet, Makhtum-kuli. The Emir's rich gifts were also mentioned on the occasion of the journey undertaken in 1890 by an Italian prince, the future King Victor-Emmanuel III[103]. Usually, Europeans and Russians got rid of these numerous gifts during the remainder of their travels or sold them at the bazaar, in the very place where they were bought by the furnishers of the Court of the Emir, before they were again offered to the next visitors. "The general maxim in Central Asia is to have one's hand open at all times in order to receive or to give; in other words, never to be stingy is an exigence of the habits of the country"[104].

47. Harnesses and other iron objets for horses, 1871-1872. Anonymous photographer.

Making systematic and planned collections for Museums on research expeditions (in Russia they were usually organized by the Russian Geographical Society, the Russian Committee for the Study of Central, Eastern Asia or by the Society of Friends of Natural History, Anthropology and

48. Harnesses and saddles, 1871-1872.
Anonymous photographer.

Ethnography and by the Museums themselves, especially the Kunstkamera). Besides the well-formed specialists sent to Central Asia, the Museum of Anthropology and Ethnography (the Kunstkamera), for example, began to prepare non-specialist amateurs by organizing lectures in ethnology and guided tours of these collections, by providing them with a booklet of directions which had been prepared by V.V. Radlov "Instructions for the collecting of ethnographical objects, related to the daily life of the Kirghiz in the Steppes General Governorship" (Saint-Petersburg, 1898). Amateurs welcomed this kind of information on the gathering of collections. Thus, the Head of the Lepsinsk district, K.N. de Lazari, wrote in 1898 to D. Klements, director of the Kunstkamera: "I am pleased to be the correspondent of the Museum and I shall try to respond accurately and rigorously to all the orders and questions coming from the Museum [...]. I request the furnishing of the most detailed instructions about the kind of information of importance to the Museum on the life of the Kirghiz, which points I should focus on, and which aspects are to be described?"[105].

It is worth pointing out that later, in the 1920s and 1930s, the scientific expeditions sent out by the Museums often used the clothes offered by the Emirs of Bukhara and clothes belonging to the old collections for exchange purposes in order to compile new collections[106].

***

In summary, we can conclude that the genesis of collecting methods (with the exception of natural collections which are not taken into consideration in the following analysis[107]) started in the late 1860s with military seizures, contributions and gifts. In the 1870s these methods were supplanted by the illegal collecting of architectural facing and archaeological objects during private archaeological excavations and explorations. The latter gradually ceased as a result of efforts made by the Russian Imperial Archaeological Committee, giving way, by the 1890s, to legal purchasing from antiquarian and traditional markets and directly from artisans, and to the collecting of material on research expeditions organized by museums or scientific societies.

10. Export of the Collections and Collectors' Motives

After the Russian conquest, Turkestan was regarded as a part of Russia's internal market (the metropolis and the colony constituted one geographical and political unit). Therefore, even if the problem of exporting collections to Russia was discussed in the local press, with protests levelled against the concentration of "antiques" in the capitals, i.e. in Tashkent, Saint-Petersburg and Moscow (V.L. Vyatkin and M.N. Rostislavov constantly called for the foundation of an archaeological museum in Samarkand), the debate was never as heated as that on the export of Central Asian collections from the Russian Empire.

As a rule, Central Asian antiques were brought to Europe and then to America via "antikachi", the booksellers and tradesmen of

49. Jewish silk merchants, by Zarifov, 1923.

Turkey, India, Persia and Russia. The main export artery was the traditional route, i.e. the Trans-Caspian railway and, from there, the roads through Turkey, Persia or Russia. Another, less popular and far more dangerous route for the tradesmen, ran through Afghanistan and India. V.L. Vyatkin and A.A. Polovtsev attest a sort of ethnic specialization of dealers in the export system, which was well-established by the 1880s. For example, with regard to manuscripts, Afghan traders worked for the Indian, and, consequently, for the British market; Armenians, Turks, Jews and Iranians supplied the European and American markets with goods mostly via Persia, though often the latter would bring old manuscripts to their home libraries[108]. General A.V. Komarov, in a letter to Count A.A. Bobrinsky, President of the Imperial Archaeological Committee, noted that "all of the coins, tableware and other discoveries from the Trans-Caspian Region are sold to Persia by Jews and Armenians"[109].

On the other hand, Europeans travelling around Turkestan could find plenty of 'sources' from among the native population for enriching their collections. Likewise, the Russian inhabitants were a good source for the collections of foreigners: J. Chaffanjon bought a collection from L.S. Barszscewski; a certain "Bastian" bought a collection of objects from N.P. Ostroumov for the Berlin Museum

50. The Turkestan Governor-General K.P. von Kaufmann. Anonymous photographer.

of Ethnography, which the Tashkent Museum had refused to purchase, calling them "uninteresting rubbish"[110]. The situation provoked strong protests from among the Russian élite, and numerous scholars from Saint-Petersburg and Moscow, although it was quite clear that "it is impossible to nip the evil in the bud in the present situation"[111].

A different point of view was held by V.V. Bartold, who was rather pessimistic about the possibility of creating a system for preserving artistic and historical heritage in Turkestan, and considered it quite natural that the interests of rather abstract "world scholarship" prevailed over local ambitions: "As long as unimpeded and irreversible pillage of historical objects goes on, we can only welcome foreign scholars and museum agents, or even tourists purchasing them, for sooner or later, their collections may come to museums or be made accessible to scholars by the owners"[112]. To some extent Bartold was right, for the majority of private collections later became part of national collections, forming the basis both of large museums in Central Asia[113] and oriental departments in museums, libraries and archive centres in Russia, Europe and America.

As for the reaction of the Russian administration, it was rather ambivalent: on the one hand a ban was imposed on archaeological excavations and the export of collections but, while applying to some foreign travellers, others were given the official permission of the Russian Imperial Archaeological Committee to conduct archaeological research[114] and take collections abroad. On the other hand, the administration would sometimes facilitate the collecting and transportation of objects (providing special carriages for transporting them through Turkestan[115], military escorts and geographical and topographical maps made by the Russian Head Quarters[116]; allowing them to take the collections abroad duty-free[117] or donating collections to western museums[118]). Ch.-E. Ujfalvy, under the patronage of the Turkestan Governor-General, K.P. von Kaufmann, was allowed to travel freely all over Russian Turkestan, escorted by military officials. Later he wrote: "If I could move freely all over Turkestan, if I could visit every part of it, if I knew all about the goings-on of the Russian administration, if I could see this oft slandered administration working closely together with the native population, it was all thanks to the extraordinary benevolence of General von Kaufmann... It is true that Russian colonization is very much like Roman colonization, but the Russians are as hospitable as the Arabs"[119].

It appears that a positive solution to this problem has yet to be found even today. The problem of collecting and exporting collections, both legally and illegally, is inextricably linked to a series of legal, moral and philosophical questions, revolving around the idea of cultural heritage, the right to private property (often legally dependent on the sale of property), the national interests of a state, and the need to preserve monuments and to make them accessible for study purposes. It is also connected with the unstable relations between metropolis and colony or homeland and foreign land.

Moreover, the situation has been further complicated by the fact that many collections were donated or sold to Russian and foreign museums by native collectors or dealers of Turkestan (Hafiz, Khodji-zargar, Zampayev, Sarger, Ju.K. Kazbekov, Mîrzâ Barat Mullâ Kasymov, G.A. Shamsutdinov, Akram Palvan Askarov, A. Kichi Kul-Ogly, I. Muhammedov, N. Nurseitov, M.U. Musakhanov, Yusupov, and others). They were not only motivated by financial interests, thus, Mîrzâ Bukhari, one of the most active donators, was inspired by the desire to make antiques in his homeland accessible for study purposes ("I do my best for the common good and for Russia's scholars") and to preserve them in good condition ("from the earliest times the Russians have preserved all noteworthy things, and we have not preserved anything to remind

51. Samarkand. Shah-i Zindah, 1871-1872. Anonymous photographer.

52. Mausoleums in Old Merv (15th century), by Kohl, after a photograph, 1880s.

us of the times of the Khans; after the death of a Khan various things passed on to private persons and no one took care of preserving them for future generations")[120].

The desire to preserve an intact image of Turkestan's early way of life actually materialized through the compiling of collections implying that they had to be exported for study purposes. This antagonistic fact resulted in an ambiguous feeling common to every foreigner, be he Russian or European. Thus, the Head of the Lepsinsk district, K.N. de Lazari, wrote: "After the construction of the Trans-Siberian Railway, whose single branch will soon cross our district, the Kirghiz way of life will quickly be overthrown. Therefore, it seems to me that a complete image of today's nomadic life must be urgently constructed. I would like to take numerous photographs for the Museum [Kunstkamera] and for this purpose I shall not husband my strength, nor my personal means". Elsewhere he added that he was also prepared to compile the necessary collections and to send them to Saint-Petersburg[121].

Even if the purpose of their activities in the name of science was faultless, collectors avoided psychological stress by extending their collections in such a way that they were protected from any future critics. Thus, the French traveller, Marie Ujfalvy-Bourdon, wrote of an unusual readiness, on the part of the custodians of mosques in Turkestan and Samarkand, to sell fragments of architectural decoration to people interested in them: "As true vandals, but with the purpose of our mission in mind [the first French scientific expedition to Central Asia], we take apart the bricks which seem to easily come apart. This is regarded as a scandal and is lamented by the old mullâs, but their scruples vanish with the appearance of the roubles which Mr. de Ujfalvy offers them"[122].

This problematic situation, which was already explosive in the 19th century, still remains delicate in the early 21st century, making the world balance practically between two extremes: acknowledgement of the status quo of the distribution of things of artistic value in the world, resulting from the "deportation of national heritage", or their compulsory redistribution, i.e. restitution[123]. The demand for the return of national heritages, the principle of which is morally defendable, but – even today – continues to provoke scepticism among museum curators, especially in the light of recent events in

Afghanistan or in Irak and the dispersion of antiques, which has affected other countries in the area since the opening up of new markets in 1991.

11. Location of the Collections

In Russia, for example, at the dawn of the 20th century, most of the Central Asian collections were concentrated in Moscow:

– a) The Armoury of the Kremlin; – b) the Dashkova Ethnographic Museum (founded as a museum of decorative and applied arts in 1867 by the Society of Friends of Natural History, Anthropology and Ethnography, established in 1863 at the Moscow University; after 1917 it was called the Museum of Ethnology, and since 1934 – the Moscow Museum of the Peoples of the USSR; its collections were transferred to the Museum of Ethnography of Saint-Petersburg in 1948); – c) the Moscow Polytechnical Museum ; – d) the Museum of the Society for the Promotion of Arts;

and in Saint-Petersburg: – a) the Saint-Petersburg Public Library; – b) the Asiatic Museum; – c) the Russian Museum (in 1934 the State Museum of the Ethnography of the Peoples of the USSR was organized on the basis of its Ethnographical Department; it is now in possession of 194 collections with a total of 8,821 objects and 99 collections of photographs including 5,255 items[124]); – d) the Armoury of Tsarskoye Selo (with the Khivan treasure donned by K.P. von Kaufmann in 1876[125]); – e) the Museum of Baron Stiglitz' Art School.

The largest Central Asian collection was in the possession of the Hermitage, where it was exhibited in three rooms: – a) "the Saddle Room" with Turkish and Bukharan saddles, ossuaries and terracotta bought by N.I. Veselovsky in Samarkand in 1883-1895 (including the collections of Mîrzâ Bukhari, Yusupov and Sarger) and discovered by V.V. Bartold at the excavations of Afrasiab in 1904; – b) "the Room of Oriental Antiques" with the carved wooden doors of Gur-Emir, fabric from a Nestorian burial ground in Semirechye, bronze mirrors of Chinese origin, ceramic fragments from various periods, objects of chased copper, Central Asian arms, objects captured during the Khivan Expedition of 1873, the gifts of the Emir of Bukhara, 1910-1911, and some things bought from

J.-A. Castagné, M.V. Stolyariov and V.L. Vyatkin; – c) "the numismatic department" where, among various other collections, those of V.V. Velyaminov-Zernov and General Komarov were exhibited[126].

The Kunstkamera in Saint-Petersburg also housed an important collection (in 1956 it had about 5,000 specimens in all), mostly collected on special expeditions. Some of these collections have been exhibited since 1891 by the Ethnographical Museum of the Russian Geographical Society[127]; some objects have been bought from collectors, others have been offered. After the Revolution (1917) the nationalized collections were usually dispersed on the orders of the State Museum Fund [*Gosudarstvennyj Muzejnyj Fond*]. Thus, the Kunstkamera was enriched by private collections, such as those in the Museum of Baron Stiglitz' Art School[128] and Pushkin's Home (Institute of Russian Language and Literature of the Academy of Sciences), which included some objects belonging to the family of Count Abamelek-Lazarev (1924)[129] and Count N.D. Romanov (1924)[130].

This practice is omnipresent. In the period 1918-1920 the State Museum of History in Moscow also received 250 Central Asian items from the State Museum Fund[131]. In 1922 the State Museum of Ethnography received ten Turkmenian carpets from the Palaces of Gatchina and Peterhof[132]. In 1924 the Hermitage received the "Khivan Treasure" from the Armoury of Tsarskoye Selo (more than a hundred specimens collected by K.P. von Kaufmann in 1873) and in 1925 some collections from the Museum of Baron Stiglitz' Art School. In Moscow the Museum of the Peoples of the USSR received A.A. Bobrinsky's collection made in 1900 at Darvaz and E.E. Pirlik's collection compiled in 1916 in Eastern Bukhara[133]. The Museum of Oriental Cultures was created in 1918 using the collections received from the State Museum Fund[134].

The sharing of collections not only enriched Russian museums, but also Central Asian ones, like, for instance, the Museum of History in Tashkent and the Museum of Samarkand, to which many items were transferred from the State Museum Fund.

In Europe, the most important collections were concentrated in France and in Germany.

In France, the Turkestan collections were concentrated in the Ministry of Public Instruction, and then distributed among the col-

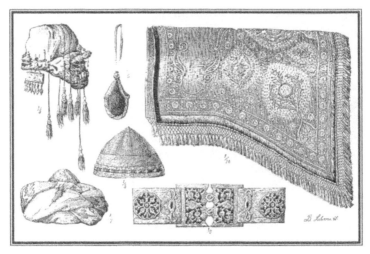

53. Textiles and ornaments of Ch.-E. Ujfalvy's collection, 1880s.

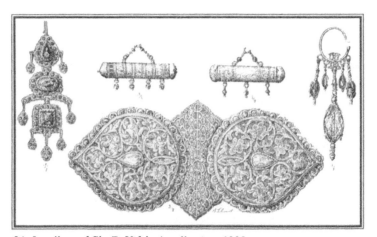

54. Jewellery of Ch.-E. Ujfalvy's collection, 1880s.

lections of Trocadéro, the Library of the Asiatic Society, the Museum of Natural History, and the Guimet Museum (Paris). Later, when the Guimet Museum was transformed from the *Museum of religions* into the *Asiatic Museum*, an attempt was made to base all of the Asian collections there, although it was not such a success[135].

Since the beginning of the 20th century, many collections have been distributed throughout the world. One of the best examples is

Ch.-E. Ujfalvy's collection, which was divided among – a) the Museum of Man in Paris (le Musée de l'Homme, Trocadéro), which took over the greater part of it, including the entire collection of enamelled tiles; – b) the Cabinet of Medals of the National Library of France, which all the traveller's numismatic collections were transferred to; – c) the private collection of Charles Schefer, a Member of the Institute of France and Director of the School of Modern Oriental Languages; – d) the collection of the Anthropological Society of Paris (craniological material), – e) the Archaeological Museum of Saint-Germain-en-Laye (218 objects made of bronze and iron from the burial mounds in Karelia[136]) and the Museum of Ethnography of the University of Bordeaux II. It may be assumed that part of the collection remained in the possession of the collector[137].

Today, only some of the collections are known, which were brought to Europe and America in the latter half of the 19th and early 20th century:

France: The Museum of Man in Paris (Musée de l'Homme, Département Asie du laboratoire d'ethnologie) has ethnographical collections (1880-1896), made by Ch.-E. Ujfalvy, Baron de Baye, P. Labbé, Mourier and J. Martin. Some of the items from the collections belonging to Ch.-E. Ujfalvy, H.-R. d'Allemagne, E. Blanc and E. Hindamian are on display in the Museum of Fine-Arts in Lyon, in the Louvre (in the Department of Moslem Antiques in the Louvre) and in the Museum of Ethnography of the University of Bordeaux II. H. Krafft's collection is deposited at the Musée-Hôtel Le Vergeur in Reims (carpets, ethnographical objects and photographs). Other deposits are to be found in the Guimet and Cernuschi Museums.

The manuscripts constitute an important part of the collections. Some have been donated to the Bibliothèque Nationale[138]:

– a) two Persian manuscripts were donated by P. Aubry (in 1902); – b) J.-A. Decourdemanche, in whose residence at Sarcelles there was a collection of coins and manuscripts, which he had acquired on trips to Istanbul, Odessa and Egypt (with some copies, perhaps made in the East on his orders), and donated to the Bibliothèque Nationale in 1908[139]; – c) E. Blanc donated 35 manuscripts[140]; – d) in 1908 Commandant Ch. A. M. d'Ollone

55. H. Moser's collections at Charlottenfeels, in Schaffhausen, 1910.

donated his collection, which he had compiled in Chinese Turkestan[141].

Other deposits have been identified: – a) some manuscripts stitched together in the 18th century, originally belonging to Silvestre de Sasy. On his death they came into the possession of E. Quatremère, and later, in 1858, they were donated to the National Library in Munich[142]; – b) the collection of E. Nathan Adler based

56. H. Moser's collections at the Museum of History of Bern, 1990.

in the Jewish Theological Seminary in New York (manuscripts).

Germany: – a) the Gottfried Merzbacher collections at the *Museum für Völkerkunde* in Munich (classified and catalogued for the first time by L.A. Chvyr') are among the numerous private collections in Munich[143]. They belong to the remaining Central Asian collections in European museums, and comprise adornments partly from the middle of Central Asia (Samarkand, Bukhara and Tashkent) and partly from nomadic regions. Collections of Turkmen objects are deposited at the *Museum für Völkerkunde* in Leipzig[144], and in W.R. Rickmers' collection at the Ethnographical Museum in Berlin (ethnographical objects and photographs). The other collections, relating to Central Asia as a whole, including Chinese Turkestan and the Tibetan area, are deposited in the Ethnographical and Indian Museums of Berlin, in the archives of the Academy of Sciences of Berlin-Brandenburg, at the Übersee-Museum in Bremen, the Ethnographical, German and Alpine Museums in Munich, and in the library and archives of the federal state of Bavaria (Staatliche Sammlungen).

As regards *other countries*, the most important collections are as follows: – a) H. Moser's Collection in the Historical Museum of Bern (arms, harnesses, clothes, fabrics, jewellery, ceramics, manuscripts – some 4,000 items in total, and some albums of photographs); – b) O. Olufsen's Collection at the National Museum in Copenhagen (over 700 items, mostly ethnographical objects, as well as some specimens of rock paintings); – c) a collection of Moslem art at the Medelhavsmuseet, in Stockholm, made by Fredrik Martin and Carl-Johan Lamm; – d) some objects from R. Pumpelly's excavations in Anau are in the *Museum für Völkerkunde* in Berlin (bronze arrow-heads) and at the University of Bern; – e) the collection and library (690 volumes) belonging to the Italian traveller, F. de Filippi, is now at the Istituto Geografico Militare di Firenze, and there is another Central Asian collection in the Museum of Ethnography in Florence; – f) America is represented by the E. Schuyler's ethnographical collection and museums such as the Nelson Gallery in Kansas-City, the Peabody Museum of Archaeology and Ethnology and the Fogg Art Gallery in Cambridge (Mass.); – g) some rather curious objects (mostly fragments of architectural facing and ceramics) are on display at the

Victoria and Albert Museum in London. But, undoubtedly, the most well-known object in the Central Asian collections is the so-called Treasure of the Oxus, now in the British Museum[145].

12. Discovering Central Asia through Collections

One of the results of such a policy, which must be treated with due caution at all times, was the discovery of Central Asia by the rest of the world by means of showing Turkestan collections at exhibitions, in museums and learned societies, both Russian and foreign. The desire to exhibit one's private collection, which – with a few exceptions[146] – was a natural collector's attitude, was not unusual for collectors of Central Asian antiques.

57. Grand Duke N.K. Romanov.
Anonymous photographer.

There were many ways of making a collection known to a wider audience, all of which were practised by the owners of collections in Turkestan.

Thus, in Turkestan itself, many Russian collections were organized in the form of home museums with a fixed 'in-day' (the "Turkestanians" V.L. Vyatkin, A.I. Dobrosmyslov, I.T. Poslavsky and N.K. Romanov displayed their collections in such a way)[147]. In Europe, this way of exhibiting a collection was practised by H. Moser in Switzerland, who organized a private museum at his residence in Charlottenfels, where he had spent his childhood[148].

Another possibility was to lend out objects from private collections and to exhibit them at meetings, organized by learned societies and circles (a common procedure for the Turkestanian Circle of Friends of Archaeology , the Russian Imperial Society for Oriental Studies, the Russian Imperial Archaeological Society, the

Geographical Societies of Russia, France, Belgium, Germany, etc.[149]), or even to display them at special exhibitions, either private (V.V. Vereshchagin[150], A.A. Kushakevich, N.K. Romanov, H. Moser, H. Krafft and others) or in museums or libraries. Even local collectors often presented their collections at exhibitions, sometimes at their own expense.

But the most common method was to include Turkestanian antiques in international, Russian and Turkestanian exhibitions, often organized in the colonial context[151]. Gradually they grew in number, and since the exhibition sets were usually prepared by the same people, a sort of "ready-made exhibition set" came into being, which wandered from one exhibition to another (this phenomenon was particularly characteristic of Russian and international exhibitions). One of the most frequent exhibitors was the Emir of Bukhara, who actively participated in almost every exhibition.

On the other hand, participation in these exhibitions was regarded in Russia and Turkestan as a matter of state prestige, and – for this reason – high-ranking state officials were engaged in organising them, and naturally their private collections merged with the exhibited collections. Thus, the collection of fabrics, carpets and clothes, made by Generals M.G. Chernyaev and N.L. Gondatti for the anthropological exhibition in 1867, was later incorporated into Governor-General K.P. von Kaufmann's private collection[152].

58. Grand Duke N.K. Romanov's Palace, 1932. Anonymous photographer.

59. Ch.-E. Ujfalvy's collection at the Universal Exhibition of 1878 in Paris. Anonymous photographer.

Europeans, commissioned by museums to collect objects in Turkestan, who were not anxious about representing the Russo-Asian province at exhibitions, stayed away from this "exhibition heatwave" as far as Turkestan was concerned, and remained preoccupied with their own colonies.

Exceptions to this rule were: Ch.-E. Ujfalvy, who exhibited his Turkestan ethnographical and archaeological collections and photographs at the international exhibition in Paris in 1878 (they included the atlases of anthropological, archaeological and art objects, published in the 4th, 6th and the 5th volumes of the work entitled the *French Scientific Expedition to Russia, Siberia and Turkestan*); E. Masson, who showed his collections at the Exposition coloniale of 1894 in France; H. Krafft, who prepared a special exposition at the *Union centrale des arts décoratifs*, and H. Moser, who – at his own risk – organized small exhibitions in Switzerland and France (Paris, the Panorama de Marigny, at the Champs-Elysées, 1891 and 1893).

For the Occidental society, permanently impressed by exotic curiosities, the news-papers were always a good place for advertising exhibitions: thus, when J. Chaffanjon showed his collections at the specially organized exhibition, opened in 1897 by the ministers of education, commerce and colonies in the Zoological gallery of the Muséum d'histoire naturelle, a wide range of papers devoted space to the event. The *Petit journal* wrote: "Chaffanjon's exposition includes a considerable number of objects: ornamented ceramics from the excavations of Afrasiab, [...] a collection of costumes, embroidery, 2,000 specimens of plants, 150 species of mammals, 800 birds, an innumerable collection of insects and numerous photographs. Let us mention, at random, some of the most interesting objects: a rich Sarte ornament, an embroidered and dyed fabric with an amazing array of colours, an exact reproduction of the inscription on Tamerlan's grave made of fabric, a series of Sarte costumes, often with inlays, Buryat and North Mongolian costumes, fragments of figurines and sarcophagi of great artistic value, small cone-shaped vessels for the ashes of the deceased... a stone pedestal for praying, embellished with the words of a Koranic surah [...], a Mongolian jurt"[153].

Collectors of Turkestanian antiques were traditionally known as benefactors. This term applied to almost all of the Russian, Central Asian and western collectors, who donated their collections or parts of them to museums. Russian[154] and western European[155] donors to museums were in abundance. Representatives of the Turkestan native population also upheld the tradition of donating collected objects to museums (e.g. the Emir of Bukhara [*Turkestanskie Vedomosti* (The Turkestanian News), 1897, N 14], A. Askarov, Mîrzâ Bukhari, L.D. Birkimbaev, Kh.I. Imambaev).

Mîrzâ Bukhari was the most important representative of the native donors, making, in 1883, a generous donation of archaeological materials to the Tashkent Museum: "two golden coins (Hebrew and Arabian) found near Bukhara; 10 Bactrian silver coins, big and small (3 found near Bukhara, the others in

60. Mîrzâ Bukhari, 1886.
Anonymous photographer.

Afrasiab in Samarkand), 5 Kufic silver coins (Afrasiab), 2 silver coins belonging to King Vasudeva (from an unknown site), 15 "Indian or Old Persian and 4 Arabian" silver coins; 96 "various copper coins" (all from Afrasiab), 5 golden rings, 31 seals and

61. Turkestanian Department at the All-Russian Manufactures Exhibition in 1870.

62. Turkestanian Department at the All-Russian Polytechnical Exhibition of 1872 in Moscow, by N. Karazin.

63. Turkestanian Department at the Universal Exhibition of 1873 in Vienna.

many other antiques"[156]. In 1888, on his way back from Saint-Petersburg, he sent 43 objects to the Emperor's Administrative Office. They were mainly found in Samarkand and Bukhara, and included 2 golden coins. On 21st October, 1888 at the request of the Imperial Archaeological Committee, which expressed its wish to see his collection, Mîrzâ Bukhari sent 6 cases of coins and other "antiques" to Saint-Petersburg (6,300 items altogether), "to be owned by the state, in exchange for a reward to be made by the Committee", but he did not fix his own prices. The Archaeological Committee bought all of the antiques he sent, except for the copper coins (only 62 were bought out of a total of 4,956). In 1889, he sent 13 gold and copper Roman, Byzantine and Mediaeval Oriental coins (identified by V.G. Tisenhausen) to the Archaeological Committee. In 1891, the Hermitage bought 11 of the terracottas, which had been sent by Mîrzâ Bukhari. In 1892 he informed the Committee that he had bought 7 more gold coins and 8 silver ones[157].

In Europe, some collectors, such as H. Krafft[158] founded their own museums or sold pieces from their collections to state museums at very reasonable prices[159]. According to S.P. Rusejkina, up to 1917, many museums in the Soviet Union derived their funds from "objects collected and donated by private collectors"[160]. This rather harmless sentence hides a sad reality: a lot of private collections, like those of the Tzar's family and aristocratic families (such as that of the Counts Abamelek-Lazarev and Bobrinsky), were confiscated and later distributed to various institutions[161].

Buying collections at auctions was comparatively rare. Among the best known examples is that of the Russian painter N.N. Karazin, who shortly before his death, had to auction off both his large collection "of various oriental things" and his own works[162].

13. The Publications of the Collections

Influenced initially by their own personal taste, in time, the collectors came to realize the importance of attributing the collected objects, describing them and interpreting them from a semantic and chronological point of view. Combined with the desire to popularise their collections, their endeavours resulted in detailed publica-

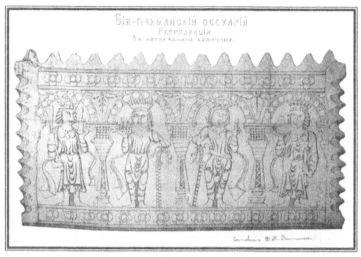

64. Ossuary of Biya-Naiman, by B.N. Kastalsky, 1909.

tions, usually pioneering ones. Among such publications was one
of the first attempts to describe and interpret the artistic decoration
of ossuaries undertaken by their owner and discoverer B.N.
Kastalsky[163].

Among the studies of I.T. Poslavsky a considerable amount of
space is devoted to the description and analysis of the objects in his
collections (notes on ossuaries, spherical and cone-shaped vases
and gems)[164]. Poslavsky put forward the idea that intaglios, described by him, served as a sort of mandate or credentials given to a
person entrusted with a mission.

S.M. Dudin attempted to reconstruct the lost art of making tiles,
of glazing, baking, and decorating them on the basis of numerous
photographs of architectural monuments in Samarkand, Bukhara,
Anau, Bairam-Ali, Ak-Serai, Shahr-i Sabz, taken by himself, and
on the basis of inquiries and personal observations. He proposed
dividing Central Asian tiles into three types: tile mosaics, majolica
tiles and relief tiles, which, in their turn, could be subdivided into
some other kinds of tiles[165]. Based on his collections he wrote
works on Central Asian carpet production[166], traditional ornament[167], a special work on Kirghiz ornament[168] (with some confu-
sion surrounding Kirghiz and Kazakh vernacular terms[169]), as well
as works on wood-carving[170] and artistic ceramics of Central Asia

(mainly from Samarkand) in which he described 300 ornamental patterns[171]. He also wrote a detailed account of the results of his collecting activities[172].

S.M. Dudin helped N.F. Burdukov collect and interpret "pieces of painted crockery". Burdukov was the owner of one of the first large-scale specialized collections of ceramics, of which he later published an account with commentaries[173].

He was also the author of quite remarkable official reports on carpet production and surveys of carpet exhibitions. With a deep understanding of the subject, due to the personal experience he had gained while travelling around Turkestan, Iran and Afghanistan as an inspector responsible for the development of traditional handicrafts and owing to his excellent knowledge of both the carpet collections of the capital's museums and his own collection, he gave reports on Turkmen carpet production in the late 19th and early 20th century[174].

Another owner of a vast collection of carpets, made during the four years of his period in office as Head of the Trans-Caspian District, General A.A. Bogolyubov, published it in a voluminous album including 662 drawings (by K.S. Mishin), representing only 139 items of his carpet collection[175], mostly Turkmen, and a Central Asian carpet production map providing information on peoples and tribes producing carpets and their location in Central

65. Karakalpak Women of Chimbay making a carpet, by K.A. Fisher.

Asia, according to which the carpets were classified and identi-fied[176]. Despite some inaccuracies when describing ornaments, colours and in dating certain specimens, much criticized by N.I. Veselovsky and A.A. Semenov[177], this work was very important in its day. Moreover, Russian scholars later adopted Bogolyubov's hypothesis that Turkmen ornament, by virtue of its antiquity, might be used as an additional source for the reconstruction of the anthro-pogenesis and ethnogenesis of the Turkmen nation and his classifi-cation of carpets has been reproduced, time and time again, in research publications.

Baron A.A. von Falkersam, who was in possession of another large collection of Central Asian carpets, started by describing his own collection and then turned to an analysis of the carpets in the hands of museums in capitals, to the study of Russian and western European works on carpets and to the findings of S.M. Dudin's research in Central Asia. As a result, he published a serious work entitled *The old carpets of Central Asia*[178], which analyses the artis-tic and technical characteristics of Central Asian carpets, gives a detailed account of Kirghiz carpets of the Ferghana valley, provides new information on the "Kashgarian" carpets of Eastern Turkestan, and deals with some theoretical questions (the origin of "national styles" in carpets, the nature of carpet ornaments, which the author, on the advice of S.M. Dudin, considers to be connected with image, and not with abstract geometrism, etc.).

Among the publications of western European collections, of special interest are those by H. Moser[179], E. de Zichy[180], E. Blochet[181] and Ch.-E. Ujfalvy[182]. The latter was also the author of one of the first scholarly publications dedicated to artistic metal-work[183].

Many works by specialists in numismatics, archaeology, ethno-graphy and ancient oriental manuscripts were devoted to objects in their collections (A.A. Divaev, E.F. Kal', N.N. Khanykov, N.S. Lykoshin, N.A. Mayev, V.P. Nalivkin, N.P. Ostroumov, A.A. Semenov, V.V. Velyaminov-Zernov, N.I. Veselovsky, V.L. Vyatkin, and others).

The native residents of Turkestan did not publish scholarly (in the real sense of the word) descriptions of their collections, giving only brief accounts of the circumstances surrounding the discovery

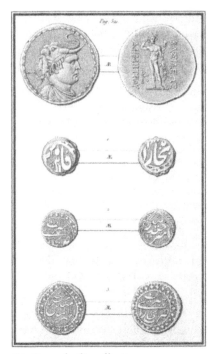

66. *Meyendorf's collection from Bukhara, 1820.*

of their "antiques" and simply listing the objects in their collections. For example, Mîrzâ Bukhari published a brief note on the purchase of the antiques found at Afrasiab in the spring of 1888: "A black stone jar with carved ornamentation and names and several lines of Arabian Kufic script on it, [...] two old mirrors made of copper, with ornaments and inscriptions, [...] several clay figurines, [...] several stone seals with images and one copper seal"[184]. Sometimes newspapers carried reports on the collections of native inhabitants[185].

There were some exceptions, though. The last kazi-kalan of Bukhara, Sadr-i Ziyâ, who was the supreme judge under Alim-khân (1910-September 1920), a poet, a patron of the arts and a bibliophile, who possessed a large library (inherited from his father and his family and enriched with his own acquisitions), copies made at his own request, and presents given on account of debts, made a catalogue of his library in Persian[186]. Prince Riza-Kuli-Mîrzâ wrote another description of private collections. According to P.P. Semenov-Tyanshanskij, in 1874 the prince joined the Amu-Darya expedition, organized by the Imperial Russian Geographical Society and led by Colonel N.G. Stoletov, and "because of his enlightened zeal for scholarship he took an active part in collecting materials, in solving ethnographical and linguistic problems, and was willing to help all those participating in the expedition owing to his knowledge of Oriental languages[187]".

Chapter III

The Central Asian Collectors

14. The Characters of the Turkestan Antiques Market

As well as antique dealers, devotees of antiques and collectors were also important characters on the antiquarian markets of Turkestan. Among them were Russian and western travellers, as well as Turkestan residents of Central Asian, Russian, western European or oriental origin. All our observations are based upon the *main body* of Russian, Western European and native Turkestan collectors, established for the period 1870-1917. They are far from being exhaustive for a number of reasons: – 1) the information about collections is sometimes very imprecise; – 2) catalogues of the collections, even if they existed, were often lost soon after the death of their owners, or – as was more often the case – did not exist at all, and therefore it is impossible to establish the exact origin and dates of some objects. Moreover, the fate of some collections is unknown; a collection, which could have had many owners, was sometimes incorporated into a new private or state collection or was distributed among several collections; we have, at best, only some fragmentary information about these changes and occasional notes in museum registers. Our analysis considers only those collections, which were mentioned in archive documents, research works and periodical publications of Pre-Revolutionary Turkestan, Russia and Europe as well as in recent publications. Some of them were not used in our analysis, especially because – for the period in question – it is difficult to distinguish between professional collecting and an amateur passion for antiques or sheer love of luxury.

Russian Collectors

It is rather difficult to distinguish between the two categories of Russian collectors in the 19th and early 20th century: the people coming to Turkestan for a certain period of time, and its permanent residents, because the first wave of Russians, migrating to Turkestan after the conquest of Central Asia, did not consider living

67. Collector Leon Barszscewski at the left of Afghan General Gulyam Khaidar-Khân, early 1890s. Anonymous photographer.

there permanently, and simply regarded their stay as a prolonged part of their career (for, in order to obtain certain ranks in the military and civil administration of Russia and to get on in one's career, it was necessary to serve in remote military provinces [Turkestan and the Caucasus]). For the Russians living in this area, from a formal point of view, the main difference between residents, temporary residents and travellers was the duration of their stay in Turkestan. Therefore, it is advisable to analyse and outline the social and professional characteristics of all of the Russian collectors who made their collections in Central Asia.

Although collecting antiques was traditionally the preserve of the aristocracy, in the period from 1870 until 1917 noblemen were rather rare among the Turkestan collectors[188]. Military officers[189], mostly generals, dominated this field. But the number of people, belonging to this social group, was steadily declining. Besides, not all "servicemen" were actively involved in military operations. Many of them were just officials, members of the diplomatic corps or engineers, but under Russian rule in Turkestan, which remained militarised throughout its existence, they were enlisted in the prestigious military department and had a military rank.

The proportion of civil officials[190], who had no military rank and were often graduates of the Oriental department at Saint-Petersburg University, amounted to about 20 % of the total number of collectors. Having joined the collecting activities after the Russian conquest of Turkestan, they continued to participate in them, and, with their numbers growing by the day, became more and more important. Eventually, after the foundation of state museums in Turkestan, many officials started to work there, thus transforming their passion for collecting into more professional activities (this happened to the Samarkand residents, V.L. Vyatkin and M.N. Rostislavov).

More than 30 % of the collectors were professional scholars[191]. The figure is impressive, especially when bearing in mind that Russia did not have so many specialists in Central Asia in the 19th and early 20th century. On the other hand, most of the scholars were working for Russian research centres and museums, and made collections for them and not for themselves (though sometimes these processes were parallel). Thus, one of the first to carry out planned collecting for the Russian museums was A.L. Kun (collections for the Museum of the Archaeological Committee, the Public Library in Saint-Petersburg, the Dashkova Ethnographic Museum and for the Moscow Society of Friends of Natural Sciences, etc. – manuscripts, numismatical, archaeological and ethnographical objects). Later the Dashkova Ethnographic Museum entrusted O.A. Fedchenko and Count A.A. Bobrinsky with the task of collecting materials connected with the culture and everyday life of the highland Tajiks (architectural and ethnographical collections, mostly embroidery and knitted things made of wool). N.I. Veselovsky and N.N. Pantusov collected archaeological materials for the Imperial Archaeological Committee. A.A. Polovtsev sent specimens of Asiatic tiles and 14th-15th century carved stucco to the museum of Baron Stiglitz' art School. In the 1890s, the Ethnographical department of the Russian Museum (later the Museum of Ethnography of Saint-Petersburg) sent the artist S.M. Dudin to Central Asia to collect ethnographical and architectural materials (metalwork, carpets, silk fabric, jewellery, architectural ornaments and decorative fragments [e.g. the carved door of the Mausoleum of Gur-Emir]). The Turkestan residents, N.P. Ostroumov, V.F. Oshanin, M.N. Rostislavov, M.V. Stolyariov, V.L. Vyatkin, and others, were engaged in the constructive collecting of materials for Turkestan and Russian museums. The most systematic work on collecting manuscripts was carried out in the Asian museum and the Public Library of Saint-Petersburg (V.V. Bartold, V.V. Grigoryev, V.A. Ivanov, A.L. Kun, N.N. Khanykov, P.I. Lerch, A.A. Semenov, V.V. Velyaminov-Zernov, N.I. Veselovsky). Sometimes museums addressed the population directly, as did the Museum of Anthropology and Ethnography of the Academy of Sciences in 1895 when it published, in the newspaper, *Turkestanskie Vedomosti* [The Turkestanian News, N° 64], a list of things which it was interested in buying ("architectural ornaments, sculptures, drawings, pictures, traditional works of art, albums of ornaments of various techniques, manuscripts, books and book bindings"). But this practice failed to yield any positive results.

Writers[192] and artists[193], who were not uncommon among the visitors to Turkestan[194], constituted no more than 7 % of the total number of Russian collectors and were usually only occasional collectors. Perhaps the reason for this was the fact that artists, who paid due attention to exotic Turkestan, were more interested in their own creative activities than in

68. The artist V.V. Vereshchagin.

buying and collecting things already made, although from the 1890s onwards some expeditions, organized specifically for the purpose of collecting, were joined by both professional artists and specialists in the humanities (V.V. Bartold and S.M. Dudin in 1893-1894, N.I. Veselovsky and N.N. Shcherbina-Kramarenko in 1895).

However, for those writers whose texts seldom went beyond simple "travel literature", "antiques" were merely "souvenirs".

Western European Collectors

The history of Turkestan collections in Europe and America is inextricably connected with the history of voyages undertaken by Europeans and Americans (potential collectors) to Turkestan. However, Turkestan failed to become a important place for tourists on a pilgrimage, and the main focus of research for scholars in the latter half of the 19th and the early 20th century. On the other hand, although Russian Turkestan was still considered a "staging post"[195], it could not avoid the tourist "boom" when people started to tire of the "old Europe" and started searching instead for a more naive and purer civilization. It is difficult to estimate the number of foreigners travelling through Turkestan precisely, but relative statistical data can be deduced from information from the Bukharan Emirate, which enjoyed the status of a Russian protectorate.

To visit the emirate of Bukhara one had to have special permission, granted at many different levels. An application for permission was first considered by the Asian Department of the Russian Ministry of Foreign Affairs, then by the Office of the Governor-General of Turkestan and then it went to the archives of the Russian Imperial Political agent in Bukhara. Not one single European, wishing to be received by the emir (which was an important destination in the travellers' itinery), could evade registration at the Russian Political Agency. One of the reasons for this was very banal: the emir only had interpreters from Russia at his disposal; but the international language of the day was French, which was always spoken by high-ranking Russian officials. Besides, according to the Russian-Bukharan Treaty of the protectorate, all of the emir's international contacts were to be controlled by Russian officials. This strict order led to the archives of the Russian Political Agency in Bukhara becoming more compact and systematic, and generally better organized, and thus more useful for an analysis of the number of western European travellers who visited Turkestan in the late 19th century. This data is, of course, relative because – 1) the documents we had at our disposal only referred to the period 1890-1898 and only to the Bukharan Emirate; – 2) sometimes the

69. The French travellers Jean Chaffanjon,
Louis Gay and Henri Mangini,
by Bellingard, 1894.

permission to travel did not mention the exact purpose of the stay in Turkestan; – 3) some of the documents, relating to the foreigners' stay in the eastern provinces of Russia, may well have been lost. But documents such as "Reports on Foreign Citizens Who Visited Bukhara and the Central Asian Provinces" and "About The Admission of Foreigners to Turkestan and the Trans-Caspian Region and the System of Granting Them Permission" enable us to draw some conclusions about the general situation.

While in the first half of the 19th century (1800-1850) only 36 men visited Central Asia, in the 1890s alone there were 289 (not to mention the numerous tourists, who were not registered by name, but only under the name of their guide, with a brief mention of their approximate number). Among the foreigners travelling around the Bukharan Emirate and Turkestan in the period, 1890-1898, there were: 75 Englishmen, 70 Germans, 57 Frenchmen, 24 citizens of Austria-Hungary, 15 Americans, 7 Danes, 4 Belgians, 4 Italians, 3 Swiss and 1 Spaniard[196].

The true purpose of these journeys is either only vaguely mentioned in the documents or is not mentioned at all. However, from the size of the groups, we may assume that the main aim was tourism (the tourist groups consisted of over 30 men[197] including schoolchildren[198] and graduates[199]), and the possibility of an exotic hunt (in 52 permits, tourism and hunting were quoted as the main purpose of the trip).

These trips were followed by trips specifically for research purposes (41), the majority of them being of a naturalist nature (28), which mainly implied research in the field of geology, geography, palaeontology, botany and zoology. Research in the field of the humanities (linguistics, history, archaeology, architecture, the history of art and ethnography), which often included some investigations into natural history, was the subject of only 13 of the trips. It should be noted that 8 out of 13 travellers were banned from doing archaeological research in the area from the very beginning[200].

Commercial and industrial ends were seldom mentioned among the purposes of the journeys (18 mentions of economic purposes); religious missions being least frequent – only 4 cases in the period discussed.

Turning to another group of archive sources[201] and to previous publications we find data on foreigners coming to Turkestan. The number of foreigners registered on their arrival to Turkestan (more 600 between 1840 and 1920[202]) is distributed unequally over the decades.

The number of travellers increased significantly after the beginning of the construction of the Trans-Caspian railway (1880), reaching its peak in 1890s, partly due to the international exhibitions held in Tashkent in 1890 and 1896, which European admirers fond of exotic things flocked to. They were attracted by the beauty of traditional Central Asian art, which was to be seen in the Russo-Asian pavilions in Paris in 1867, 1878 and 1889[203].

Here it is worth mentioning the data provided by A.M. Matveev[204], according to which the population of Turkestan, included 17,710-20,220 temporary and permanent residents from 1905 to 1917. Thus, from March to September 1917, there were 9,000-10,000 Poles, 8,000-8,500 Germans, 600-1,000 Greeks, 100-120 Czechs and Slovaks, 100 Bulgarians, 80-100 Frenchmen and

70. H. Moser, by M.E. van Muyden, 1880s.

Swiss, 50-60 Scandinavians, 60-70 Italians, 50-60 Englishmen, 20-25 Belgians and over 40,000 Austro-Hungarian and German prisoners of war[205].

If we combine data, obtained from Bukharan documents – omitting possible traders, businessmen and missionaries – with the average number of foreign travellers and residents in Turkestan, estimated according to official data from the early 20th century, we can estimate the number of collections (perhaps consisting of some "souvenirs") made by western travellers.

But leaving hypotheses behind us, and turning to documental evidence, we have to admit that precise data on western collections and collectors is rather scarce. As for the professional and social background of the foreign collectors of Turkestanian antiques known today, the vast majority of them were professional researchers[206] (though some of them had military ranks[207]) engaged by state institutions for exploratory expeditions to Central Asia and for collecting various objects for European and American Museums[208].

At the same time, among the western collectors travelling in Turkestan, there were amateur admirers of antiquity, engaged by various private and public enterprises[209], adventurers[210] (including businessmen[211]), artists, who were engaged in making a collection of their own drawings[212], photographers[213], collectors – whose social and professional status is very difficult to identify[214] – and, of course, diplomats[215], as well as noblemen[216].

Central Asian Collectors

Among the native population of Central Asia *anticomania* was due to a strong Russian and European influence, for – according to the Iranist A.A. Semenov – before the Russian conquest, the native residents "had not been infected with treasure-hunting"[217]. Their collections included ancient manuscripts, Persian miniatures, "girikhs" (stencils of architectural ornaments)[218] and Chinese porcelain, although we should not forget the artisans' collections of objects, traditionally manufactured by their family clans and guilds, and, of course, the treasures of the Central Asian khans, e.g. the description of the treasury of Khivan khan, by the American journalist MacGahan in 1873, reproduces a marvellous image of the caves of the Ali-Baba where, among numerous magnificent carpets, one came across heaps of arms ("knights' gloves with lilies", richly decorated oriental guns, "Khorasan steel arms, Persian sabres and thick Afghani daggers in precious sheaths, decorated with precious stones") together with a remarkable – "over 1,000 objects" – collection of the Chinese and Russian porcelain stored in the harem[219].

In spite of the rather critical views of Countess P.S. Uvarova, the President of Moscow's Archaeological Society, who wrote in 1891, after her trip in 1890, that the native inhabitants "collect antiques out of curiosity, sometimes trading in them, but usually just storing them, being unable to appreciate them properly and having no real interest in them"[220], a true taste for collecting gradually developed among the local élite, including members of the aristocracy and the Emir of Bukhara himself (see H. Moser's description), religious leaders and numerous representatives of the merchant class[221]. The presence of people really interested in history and archaeology is illustrated by the fact that the Turkestanian

71. Khivian Emir, by H. Moser, 1880s.

Circle of Friends of Archaeology counted - between 1895 and
1917, especially in the period just after its creation - a certain number of Asiatic members[222]. Still, for most of the population, the passion for history and collecting antiques remained an exception
rather than the rule. N.I. Veselovsky, who held an important posi-
tion, referred to this situation: "Some natives (merchants or zar-
gars) continue to make collections in the hope of fobbing one of the
Russians off with them"[223].

Taking into consideration the scanty data on Central Asian col-
lectors, we should not forget to mention a merchant from Tashkent,
Akram Palvan Askarov[224], a merchant belonging to the second
guild and the owner of the Samarkand silk, wool, and cotton facto-
ry, Mîrzâ Abdullah Bukhari[225], "Sart" Hafiz, Zampayev, Zarger,
Ju.K. Kazbekov, Mîrzâ Barat Mullâ Kasymov[226], G.A.
Shamsutdinov, Junusov, the Bukharan collector of antiques,
Muhammed Vef, the Chormanov who donated an important collec-

tion, connected to the Kazakhs, to the Kunstkamera via S.M. Dudin[227], and all those engaged in collecting antiques and ethnographic objects for Russian museums[228]: Ashir Kichi Kul-Ogly of Kyzyl-Arvat (women's silver ornaments of the Turkmen tribes of the Yomuds, Kyzyl-Arvat, 1909)[229], Bukharan Isa Muhammedov (collections of embroidery, fabrics and leather works for the Ethnographical Department of the Russian Museum, made in 1910 in Bukhara, now on display in the State Museum of Ethnography in Saint-Petersburg[230]), a teacher from the Akmola Region of Nurdjakul Nurseitov (a collection of 9 objects, common in the everyday lives of cattle-breeders in the Petropavlovsk District of the Akmola Region, 1910)[231], Kory Said Omarov of Samarkand, who was commissioned by the Samarkand Museum to buy manuscripts and coins in Bukhara in 1875, Aryngazy Khankhozhin, who – together with Chingiz Ch. Valikhanov – made a collection of 350 objects in the Kokchetava and Karkarala Districts of the Akmola Region (in the 1870s)[232] and Lankjan D. Birkimbaev and Khassan I. Imambaev who collected more than 50 items, including a Kirghiz bridal gown, for the Kunstkamera[233].

It must be noted that, while engaged in collecting things, many Turkestanian collectors, who either visited Russia themselves or were employed as correspondents by the Russian Imperial Archaeological Committee[234], followed the advice of Russian experts (e.g. Akram Palvan Askarov and Mîrzâ Bukhari were on good terms with N.I. Veselovsky, a professor at the Saint-Petersburg University, and an expert in the history of the Scythians, who generously offered them historical literature).

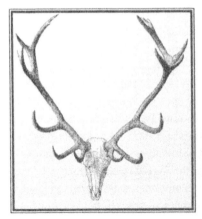

72. Deer antlers,
by M.E. van Muyden, 1880s.

73. Naturalistic plate.
Turkestanskij sbornik.

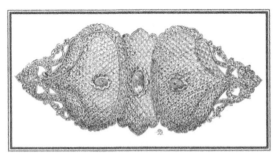

74. Buckle of belt, by M.E. van Muyden, 1880s.

Chapter IV

Description of the
Central Asian Collections

15. The Character of Central Asian Collections

Specialized or Universal ?

The character of Central Asian collections made in the latter half of the 19th and the early 20th century is distinguished by its universality (and, in this respect, they may be compared to the New World collections): everything connected with the field of "antiquity" and with the European idea of the "exotic" or everything enriching the knowledge of this remote region, was worth collecting. This is why Turkestan collections, aiming at satisfying the whole spectrum of human curiosity, included both *Naturalia* and *Artificialia*, and combined them depending on the collector's individual taste.

This situation reflects the character of the early stages of the study of Turkestan, when everything (nature, history, social life) seemed equally interesting in the eyes of European and Russian scientists. Very typical, in this respect, is the scientific aspect to the first explorations of Central Asia and the character of the specialized expeditions[235], as well as the structure of the Tashkent Public Museum[236], opened in 1876 on the premises of the School for Sericulture on the basis of the private collections, donated by A.I. Vil'kens, I.I. Krause. N.A. Mayev, V.F. Oshanin and Ju.D. Juzhakov[237].

The Museum had Industrial, Ethnographical, Agricultural and Archaeological (and Numismatical) Departments, and later Geographical, Anthropological (1877), Military and Historical (1903) and Arts (1919) Departments, too. The archaeological and numismatic department was described in a report on Russian museums, prepared by Countess P. Uvarova in 1887 for the 7th Archaeological Congress in Yaroslavl. Among over 200 items, she mentioned fragments of architectural facing from Samarkand monuments, archaeological objects found near Tashkent and in

Afrasiab (Samarkand), including "a huge bronze vessel" and over 2,000 coins[238].

By the 1890s (complex) universal collections including antiques and natural objects, had become comparatively rare and were more common in outlying districts than in the metropolitan areas of Russia and Turkestan. Thus, E. Markov, who travelled widely in the Volga Region, the Caucasus and Turkestan, considered the collection of the Head of the Osh District (who was also the paymaster of his batallion) to be very archaic. The apartment of this typical "Turkestanian" of the first generation of collectors, from the period immediately after the conquest, was packed with "various objects of local art and nature": stuffed birds, the heads of animals, the skins of snow leopards and tigers, minerals and herbariums as well as ethnographical objects: clothes, saddle-pack objects, "teacups in leather cases for travelling" and, of course, "all sorts of arms, both of Asiatic and Russian origin"[239].

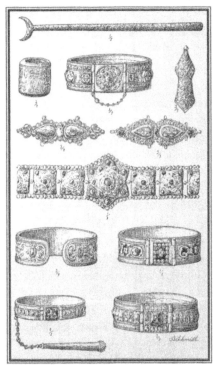

75. Sceptre, buckles, jewels and belts from Ch.-E. Ujfalvy's collection, 1880s.

However, this kind of collecting persisted much longer among professional researchers (especially among western travellers), for the results of these expensive expeditions were expected to present a full picture of the Russian Asiatic province. Jean Chaffanjon's expedition program is very typical in this respect: "to study Russian Turkestan, to collect objects of scientific and scholarly interest for national museums and to carry out historical and ethnographic research"[240].

Classical examples of such collections (excluding *Naturalia*) were those of Ch.-E. Ujfalvy[241]. Made during three successive expeditions in 1876-1877, 1879 and 1881, they included clothes, fabric, jewels, artistic metalwork, arms and musical instruments of various Central Asian peoples (especially the Galtchas), mostly bought at famous Asian bazaars (in Samarkand, Kokand, Marghilan and Tashkent) or directly from the artisans; a great number of fragments of architectural facing, e.g. the plinth of the Column of mausoleum Gur-Emir, some bricks from a country palace of Timur (perhaps Baghi-Shamal), decorative elements of the mosque of Shah-i Zinda dating back to 1354, fragments of ceramic decoration from all the medressahs of Registan (Ch.-E. Ujfalvy was especially proud of the carved stone star from the medressah of Ulugbek), some pieces of glazed facing from the mosque of Bibi-Khanym, a fragment of the cenotaph of Khodja-Ahrar; a glazed tile and a mosaic from the mausoleum of Khodja-Ahmad-Yassavi in the city of Turkestan, a brick from the ruins of Djankent; archaeological finds, such as iron and bronze objects from the excavated burial-mounds in Karelia; golden, silver and bronze coins found in Afrasiab; some fragments of ceramics, "a vase of moulded metal", a bronze ring, a fragment of burial urn and some coins from the old site covered by Lake Issyk-Kul (possibly, near Tur-Aigir), as well as coins, architectural facing and ceramics collected at the ancient sites of Pendjikent, Djankent, Ja-

76. *Copper vessels from Ch.-E. Ujfalvy's collection.*

ni-Kurgan, Kosh-Mizgile, Sena-Kurgan and Sauran, and objects from the private collections of Ivanetsky, Kaznakov, Semenov, Europoeus and Heintz representing Karelia and Siberia, photographs of Central Asian anthropological types "en face" and "de profil", and numismatic collections[242].

Of the same mixed character were the collections made between 1873 and 1900 by G. Bonvalot, E. Blanc[243], J. Brocherel, J. Chaffanjon[244], H. Moser[245], H. Krafft[246], O. Olufsen together with naturalist A. Hjuler and botanist O. Paulsen[247], H. Lansdell, W.R. Rickmers and E. Schuyler[248].

Specialized collections were extremely rare, although they appeared at the same time as universal ones[249]. Moreover, describing specialized collections as one particular group is difficult because of the scanty information available about the rest of their components, which could contradict its main specialization.

Bearing in mind the fact that in the "specialized" collections there are often categories of unreported hypothetical objects, we should not forget to mention that the first among them were the collections of N.N. Golovachev (the first numismatic collection in Turkestan) and D.L. Ivanov (hunting objects), both made in the 1860s. In the 1870s a specialized collection of musical instruments was made by A.F. Eichhorn, a military bandmaster in Tashkent in the period 1870-1883 ("string instruments of the Kirghiz and other Mongol tribes; musical instruments of the people of Turkestan, Kashgar, Kokand, Afghanistan, Bukhara and Khiva; wind-instruments of the Sarts and percussion instruments")[250]. For the 1890s we can mention, with some reservations, the "archaeological" collection of S.F. Nikolai, made in the Valley of the river Chirchik[251], and a collection of Hebrew and Persian manuscripts made by Elkan Nathan Adler in 1896-1897 in Bukhara, Samarkand and Teheran[252]. In the 1900s four partially specialized collections appeared: the carpet collections of A.A. Bogolyubov[253], Head of the Trans-Caspian District, and Baron A.A. Falkersam[254], and collections of arms made by Generals S.M. Dukhovskoy and Mishchenko[255]. The specialized collections of 1910 include collections of manuscripts made by F.F. Popelov and V.A. Ivanov (the latter was ordered by the Asiatic Museum)[256]. No specialized collections can be identified for the 1880s.

From the facts mentioned above we can conclude that the development of private collecting in Turkestan in the late 19th and early 20th century did not consist in a gradual transition from complex collections to specialized ones[257]. It would be more correct to say that what changed most was the character of universal collections, which remained complex but developed certain dominant values and preferences (archaeology, ethnography, numismatics, manuscripts, etc.), thus becoming more homogeneous.

16. Predominant Elements of Central Asian Collections

In the period in question, as Turkestan was, as far as the Russians and Europeans were concerned, an "exotic land", until recently considered *terra incognita*, *ethnographical collections*, showing the extravagance of the discovered world at its best, were predominant in the area.

Collectors paid almost the same attention to the wide variety of objects made by local artisans, which were indispensable for the traditional way of life of the native residents (clothes, fabrics, carpets, metalwork, jewellery, arms, details of interior decoration, musical instruments)[258]. It is worth noting that this mixed character was also typical of the collections made by native residents (cf. the collection of Mîrzâ Abdullah Bukhari, which included traditional silk fabric, archaeological

77. Sart woman, by M.E. van Muyden, 1880s.

78. Bukharan Emir,
by M.E. van Muyden, 1880s.

objects, numismatic sets and *girikhs*), in spite of the fact that it was Europe that was exotic for them rather than their homeland. Thus, H. Moser was surprised, too, when he saw a western European carpet adorning the throne-room of the Emir of Bukhara and the strange mixture of Russian and Oriental decorations on his uniform (military medals combined with jewellery). A. Boutroue, who visited Turkestan in 1896, was surprised to see an imitation of an interior of a Russian railway carriage in one of the rooms of the Bukharan Emir's country residence, ordered by him after his first voyage to Saint-Petersburg[259].

But in spite of this mixed character, it was not uncommon that a particular kind of ethnographical object came to be favoured by a collector, thus forming a predominant part of his collection.

As was logical in the context of the military conquest of Central Asia, *arms* were among the most preferred and widespread collector's items in the first decades after the annexation of Turkestan. They remain a predominant element of ethnographical collections up to the end of the 1870s. With some rare exceptions, collections of arms were naturally owned

79. Dagger offered by the Khivian Khan to H. Moser,
by M.E. van Muyden, 1880s.

*80. Interior of the Bukharan Emir's Palace with
a sculpture showing Peter the Great, n.d.*

by military men[260], and – according to numerous war memoirs[261] – were enriched with captured things and contributions[262]. Moreover, after the battles – as related in many memoirs– the officers bought arms from the soldiers on the cheap. On the occasion of the conquest of Khiva, "the Russian soldiers bartered bunches of Teke jewels or magnificent carpets for a bottle of vodka"[263].

When military operations in Central Asia were finally over, collecting arms as war trophies became impossible. However, other options remained: receiving arms as gifts, which also became less frequent, or buying them at markets. But high quality arms were expensive, they were handed down and as they were rarely sold at markets, the price of them increased immensely[264]. As a result, arms ceased being a dominant feature of collections, although they did not disappear from them completely, and remained an essential element of ethnographical collections. Thus, the Russian writer and traveller, V.V. Krestovsky, after a long argument about the exorbitant prices, did in fact buy ancient arms at the Embassy House in

81. Kirghiz arms of the H. Moser's collection.

Bukhara, where they had been brought on his orders by "antikachi" together with carpets, embroidered fabric, coins, Russian and Chinese porcelain and Indian metalwork[265]. The core of H. Moser's arms' collection was also formed in Bukhara.

Collections of carpets become popular in the 1880s and in the 1900's, although carpets were present in collections throughout the existence of Russian Turkestan. Carpets were preferred by collectors because of their availability and inexpensiveness in Turkestan and because they epitomized the European idea of luxury. This common idea of luxury is reflected in the description of the apartment belonging to a Russian major, the leader of the Samarkand garrison: "Like in the first room, in the rest of them there were carpets, carpets and carpets. Especially in the sitting-room: this high and spacious room is covered all over with carpets. Walls, niches, ottomans, folding stools, window-sills, floor – everything had carpets on it. It was soft, somber, tender, soundless, one feels like lolling about a bit. Indigenous shields, sabers, helmets, hauberk, jars, Chinese porcelain and other trifles are very nicely arranged everywhere"[266].

Like the collections of arms, the first collections of carpets were connected with military take-overs. According to the American journalist, MacGahan[267], who took part in the Khivan expedition of 1873, the treasury of the khan of Khiva, located in two adjoining rooms, was plundered mercilessly and partly burned, and the carpets were given to soldiers as a reward. Turkmen would sell carpets, jewellery and old ornaments at very low prices to pay their contribution. "A carpet, 30 feet long and 6 feet wide, would be sold for 25-30 roubles"[268]. Ladies' jewellery was bought by the pound: 25 roubles for a pound of silver. The same happened during the seizure of Geok-tepe, where "many could buy a carpet for a glass of vodka given to a soldier..."[269].

However, large carpet collections were not so numerous. There were no more than ten Russian carpet collections[270]. Among the western travellers, impressive collections belonged to W.R. Rickmers[271] and H.R. d'Allemagne (here it must be noted that old carpets could be taken abroad duty-free), and among the Central Asian collectors, remarkable collections belonged to the emir of Bukhara, Saïd Alim-khân (according to M.S. Andreyev this collection, overseen by a special official and his assistants, included 10,000 items: among them Central Asian, Caucasian, Iranian and European carpets).

Collections of carpets were rather similar in character. The most widespread were the cheapest Yomud strips, Kyzyl-Ayak and

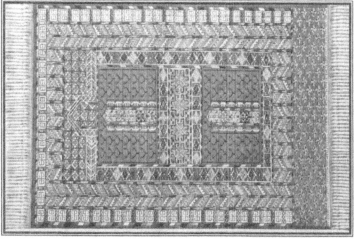

82. "Tekinian" Carpet.

Bashkir carpets, followed by "Bukharan" (i.e. Uzbek, Afghan and Belodchi) carpets. More expensive "Tekin" (Turkmen), "Salor" and "Kashgar" (i.e. East Turkestani and Indian) carpets were less common.

From the late 1880s onwards, the carpet trade begins to follow the rules of the antiquarian market, developing a certain degree of specialization. Five of the largest Russian collections of Central Asian carpets (belonging to A.A. Bogolyubov, N.F. Burdukov, A.A. Polovtsev, I.T. Poslavsky and A.A. Falkersam) were compiled by purchasing carpets, despite the rising prices. By the beginning of the 20th century, as the papers remarked, the private collecting of carpets had become virtually impossible: carpets were really

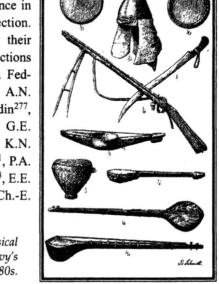

[w]eight in gold"[272], to say nothing of the numerous [app]earing on the market. But by the 1900s museums [ ] make collections of carpets. Buying carpets, for [ ]e of the aims of the trip undertaken by S.M. Dudin, [ ] Turkestan by the Russian Museum to make "eth[ ]lections" (1899-1908).

[ ]'s *Musical instruments* occasionally appeared as [ ]cialized collec[ ]it would be logi[ ]their presence in [ ]ical collection. [ ]s confirm their [ ]n the collections [ ]n[273], O.A. Fed[ ] Berg[275], A.N. [ ] S.M. Dudin[277], [ ]vsky[278], G.E. Grumm-Grzhymailo[279], K.N. Pos'et[280], I.I. Rachinsky[281], P.A. Komarov[282], A.E. Regel[283], E.E. Pirlik[284], Kartusova[285], Ch.-E.

83. Arms and musical instruments of Ch.-E. Ujfalvy's collection, 1880s.

Ujfalvy[286], H. Moser[287] and O. Olufsen[288].

ian origin were y went to the éro)[289].

84. Market of Bukhara, by H. Moser, 1889-1890.

To complete the picture, we should not forget to mention specialized ethnic collections, dedicated to the peoples of Central Asia. Much attention was paid to the Tajiks in the context of searching for the "Arian homeland", which was typical of the 19th century[290]. Tajik collections included those of A.A. Bobrinsky (architecture and ethnography of the Tajiks of Darvaz, 1898-1900)[291], A.K. Golbek (clothes of the Tajiks of Karategin)[292], I.I. Zarubin (ethnography of the Tajiks near the Pamirs and of the Western Pamirs, Rushan and Shugnan, including eleven Ismailian manuscripts, 1914-1916)[293], V.A. Ivanov (Bukhara, 1915), O.A. Fedchenko (Tajik clothes, numismatical collection and drawings), Ja.S. Edelstein (Eastern Bukhara, 1905-1910)[294], A.G. Jacobson (Tajik clothes from the Western Pamirs, 1909)[295], V.D. Pelc (Western

85. Copper vessel shop at Bukhara, 1890s. Anonymous photographer.

86. Copper vessel at Bukhara, by Hordet. 1880s.

Pamir and Samarkand, 1908-1909, 1913-1914)[296] and of the travellers G.E. Grumm-Grzhymailo (1880, 1886)[297] and A.E. Regel (1876-1885, Samarkand, Darvaz, Shugnan, Karategin)[298], G.A. Shpilko (1913-1914, 1918, Western Pamir, Murgab)[299].

Ethnographical collections representing the Kazakhs and Kirghiz were made by A.I. Dobrolyubov, A.V. Andrianov (Semipalatinsk Region, 1906; the Akmola Region, 1908)[300], P.N. Beketov (the Kazakhs of the Pavlodarsk District of the Semipalatinsk Region, 1906)[301], L.D. Birkimbaev and Kh.I. Imambaev (the Kirghiz of Turgay of the Aktyubinsk Region, 1898)[302], F.F. Karavayev (the Petropavlovsk District of the Akmola Region, 1908)[303], K.N. de Lazari, Head of the Lepsinsk District (1898, Semirechye)[304], the Curator of the Museum at Semipalatinsk, and two Frenchmen, J.M.A. de Cuverville and P. Labbé. To the same category belong the collections of A.S. Berg (ethnography of the Kazakhs, 1902, the Kazalinsk Dictrict of the Syr-Darya Region, transferred to the Kunstkamera in Saint-Petersburg)[305], V.N. Vasilyev (the Ust-Kamenogorsk District of the Semipalatinsk Region, 1916)[306], L.E. Dmitriev-Kavkazsky (Bukhara, 1905)[307], A.E. Regel (1909, Verny), N.A. Kryzhanovsky and L.F. Ballyuzek (Orenburg Kazakhs, 1870-1871)[308], K.A. Belilovsky (Turgay region)[309], Kartusova (ethnography of the Kazakhs, 1910)[310], D.D. Pedashkenko (the Semipalatinsk Region, 1906), K.M. Rychkov (ethnography of the Kazakhs, Semipalatinsk Region, 1914, 1915)[311], K.V. Shchennikov (ethnography of the Kazakhs, the Akmola Region, 1908-1909; Semipalatinsk Region, 1910)[312], who took part in the ethnographical expeditions organized by the Kunstkamera. R. von Karutz, a German, made a collection dedicated to the ethnography of the Kirghiz and Turkmen in Mangyshlak[313].

Governor-General K.P. von Kaufmann made a number of big collections dedicated to the Uzbeks (365 objects, 1870-1871, Tashkent, Samarkand, Ferghana, Chimkent; formerly the Moscow Museum of the Peoples of the USSR[314]; and 100 pieces of jewellery from Khiva, 1873, the Hermitage). Collections dedicated to the Uzbeks were those of V.A. Ivanov (Bukhara, 1916), V.D. Pelc (Samarkand and the upper reaches of the Zerafshan, 1908-1909), V. Emme (Samarkand, Ferghana)[315], F.I. Plyushkin (Bukhara, 1913-

87. Silver jewellery and other objects made by Bukharan artists, by Hordet, 1880s.

88. Coffer merchant, 1871-1972.
Anonymous photographer.

1914)[316], N.I. Tuturin (Western Pamir, 1915)[317], A.P. Fedchenko (Tashkent, 1870)[318], D.K. Trepev (Marghilan, Tashkent, Samarkand, Bukhara and Shahr-i Sabz, 1912)[319], E.E. Pirlik (Bukhara and Samarkand, 1915-1916)[320], as well as P.A. Komarov's collection of objects from the Uzbek popular puppet theatre, including libretti and photographs (Bukhara, Mangyshlak, 1906; Tashkent and Chimkent, 1907-1908)[321].

Collections dedicated to the Turkmen were made by N.N. Glushkov (Turkmen of the island of Cheleken, 1908-1909)[322], A.I. Glukhovsky (1882)[323], N.I. Grodekov (Turkmen collections of the 1880s)[324], Rotman (clothes of Yomud Turkmen from Kyzyl-Arvat and Ashkhabad, 1909, 1912)[325], M.M. Stolyariov (the 1900's)[326], and E.E. Ukhtomsky (1892)[327].

Of special interest are the collections made by S.M. Dudin who regularly visited Turkestan between 1899 and 1908 to collect objects for the Russian Museum. In these ten years alone this artist and explorer collected numerous objects, over 4,000 specimens of which were deposited in the State Museum of Ethnography in Saint-Petersburg (10 collections dedicated to the Uzbeks, 8 to the Tajiks [2 of them dedicated especially to the mountain-Tajiks], 8 to the "Sarts", 4 to the Turkmen, 3 to the Kazakhs of the Akmola and Semipalatinsk Regions and 2 to the Kirghiz) with detailed descriptions[328]. The collections of A.N. Samoilovich (ethnography of the Khivan Turkmen and Uzbeks, and the Turkmen in general, collected in the 1900's at Khiva)[329] are also worth mentioning.

The collection of religious objects made by G.A. Kolpakovsky, the collection of dervish costume made by N.N. Shcherbina-Kramarenko (Samarkand, 1909), and the collection of amulets made by B.F. Romberg (1913) were quite unique[330].

89. General G.A. Kolpakovsky, 1870s.

It is interesting to note that

90. Coppersmiths. n.d. (1920s?).
Anonymous photographer.

91. Tinman. n.d. Anonymous photographer.

many collections contain small models of ethnographical objects, because the agents working for the museums were ordered to make these models whenever it was not possible to carry large objects. This means that the earlier exotic *bibelots* have become a source of scientific information.

The ethnographical collections are followed, in second place, by the *archaeological* ones. They constantly grew in number until the 1880s, and having reached their peak in that decade – by which time they were almost comparable to the ethnographical collections in terms of number – they gradually began to decrease. Such dynamics can be explained only by the development of archaeological research in Central Asia. The need to conduct large-scale archaeological excavations in Russian Turkestan was clear to everyone. They were inspired by information gleaned from ancient and mediaeval written sources, by the magnificent ruins of architectural monuments, numerous tepe (surviving in the ancient cities), and the archaeological objects, occasionally appearing on Central Asian markets. But, owing to the lack of scholars in Russia studying Central Asia (as well as in Europe) and with priority being given to the exploration of archaeological monuments in Russia, officially authorized excavations in Turkestan, which were initially concentrated in Samarkand[331], began relatively late. At the same time, archaeological research began in other parts of Turkestan, whose results before 1895 (when the Turkestanian Circle of Friends of Archaeology was organized) could only be called promising[332] (it must be noted that it was not until the late 1920s that Central Asian archaeology really began to develop).

The pioneering explorations aroused great interest in ancient monuments and caused the inhabitants, who realized the commercial value of archaeological objects, to go on unauthorized excavations, in turn, inspiring collectors to buy the finds. On the initiative of the Russian Imperial Archaeological Committee, the government made numerous attempts to stop the unsanctioned activities. By the end of the 1880s, as the popularity of archaeological explorations continued to increase, instigated by numerous newspaper publications and the foundation of the first public museums (the Samarkand Archaeological Museum belonging to the office of the

Zerafshan District [1874], the Tashkent Public Museum [1876], the Ashkhabad Museum [1897], the East Kazakhstan Museum [1914] and the Kustanai Museum [1915]), the regulations prohibiting "injurious excavations" were tightened up. Numerous circulars (N° 229 of 4th November, 1869, N° 6 of 31st July, 1882 and N° 11 of 31st May, 1884) about the "complete prohibition of treasure-hunting"[333] issued by the Ministry of Home Affairs, as well as proclamations in the native languages published by the Imperial Archaeological Committee calling upon the inhabitants to register all of the archaeological finds and to inform the Archaeological Committee[334] about them, could not completely eradicate the evil, but reduced the number of unauthorized excavations and encouraged the handing over of occasional finds to state collections by European and native residents of Turkestan. An editorial article in the *Turkestanskaja tuzemnaja gazeta* [The Turkestanian Local Newspaper], calling upon Turkestanians to preserve the historical monuments, said: "Antiques must not be concealed, they should be published, as has recently been done by the respectable merchants of Samarkand, Mîrzâ Bukhari and Shakirdjan Ishayev"[335].

After the setting up of the Turkestanian Circle of Friends of Archaeology, the collecting of archaeological objects was far less spontaneous. At first, archaeological collections came into the hands of the Turkestanian Circle of Friends of Archaeology, and in 1899, they were transferred to the Tashkent Museum. Later, most of the finds went directly into state funds, not via private collections, which began to be donated or sold to museums far more often. After the state had announced that it was its prerogative to conduct archaeological research, Russian and foreign private collections began to disappear.

Nevertheless, we can name the largest archaeological collections.

One of the first archaeological collections was that of V.V. Vereshchagin, made mostly at the excavation of the site of Djankent (1867). It included human and animal bones, fragments of ceramics and terracotta and a "fragment of a relief inscription". All of the finds were published in the form of engravings, made by P. Alekseyev, and based on the artist's own drawings[336].

In the 1870's quite remarkable archaeological collections were made by:

– B.N. Kastalsky[337] (his first collection is meant here, see the description of I.T. Poslavsky's collection), who served for many years in Termez: 1,000 coins, among them many Sasanid gold coins; gems, one of them, found in Afrasiab, made of dark cornelian, bearing the figure of a young Hellen wearing a helmet, was identified by B.A. Turayev and S.F. Oldenburg as a Hellenistic gem depicting Alexander the Great; a carved marble panel from the site of Chupan-ata; terracotta objects and ceramics, including some fragments of the famous ossuaries from Biya-Naiman, discovered by the man himself.

– A.L. Kun (objects from his own excavations at Khodjent and the collection of Colonel Favitsky bought there; a case with archaeological finds from Tashkent, sent in 1871 to the Museum of the Archaeological Committee).

– M.N. Rostislavov, who donated his "rare collection of historical books, old manuscripts and especially the rich numismatic collection" to the archaeological museum created by himself in 1874 and attached to the Zerafshan District Office in Samarkand[338].

– Borzenkov, whose work at Afrasiab, "on one of the hills, rising steep above the river Siab", was registered as the first excavation to be conducted there, and led to the discovery of some traces of "a pottery factory" and dwelling houses, as well as some fragments of glass objects, "jars for water, large earthenware pots, tubes and other earthenware objects". After the collector's death, M.N. Rostislavov was eager to buy, his big collection of coins for the museum attached to the Zerafshan District Office[339].

– archaeological and numismatic material constituting the core of the collection belonging to the merchant, Mîrzâ Abdullah Bukhari[340].

In the 1880s, many archaeological collections were made, including some extensive and well-organized collections belonging to:

– Akram Askarov, the first Uzbek amateur archaeologist, who was awarded the Silver Medal by the Russian Imperial Archaeological Society "for the services rendered by him to archaeology"[341], i.e., for the collection of archaeological and numismatical objects and manuscripts, which according to a posthumous description written by the Archaeological Committee (D.I. Evarnitsky), consisted of 17 golden, 1,498 silver and 12,171 copper coins, "about fifty odd fragments of clay figurines of Gods", a large number of necklaces, bronze objects, jars and dishes made of silver and copper, glass vessels and 42 manuscripts[342]. Seven terracotta figurines belonging to this collection were purchased by the Museum of the Archaeological Committee, seven manuscripts were bought by the Tashkent Library, part of the numismatical collection went to the Hermitage (504 coins: 5 golden, 321 silver and 178 copper ones[343]); as for the archaeological collection, it was divided by qazis among Askarov's heirs[344].

92. Akram Palvan Askarov, 1886. Anonymous photographer.

– N.I. Veselovsky[345], who conducted the first archaeological campaign at Afrasiab in 1884-1885. It was preceded by an exploratory trip around Turkestan in 1882-1883 (excavations at the sites of Toi-tepe in the Kurama District of the Syr-Darya Region,

Chorlen-tepe near Namdanak in the Tashkent Region, Tudi-Kalyan and Tudi-khurd not far from the land of Ashtu in the Chust District; and in the Ferghana Region: Akhsy, Kasane, Uzgen, Chodak, etc.), which yielded rich ceramic and numismatical material and glass[346]. At the same time, N.I. Veselovsky would buy antiques from the inhabitants of Bukhara, Ferghana, Samarkand, Aksu and the Syr-Darya Region, e.g. in Samarkand he bought "three collections of coins and other antiques"[347] (including the ring of Miran-shah Mîrzâ, the third son of Timur, with an almond-shaped emerald, set in gold[348]). In 1883 he bought 1,202 objects from the collection of Mîrzâ Bukhari[349], from the collections of Junusov and Zarger[350], and "bought some things from poor (Baykush) people from Afra-siab and its neighbourhood" and "from Hafiz". His collection also included the gifts he had received during his stay in Turkestan[351].

– Colonel Kazantsev who donated his collection to the museum of the Zerafshan District Office and was transferred to Tashkent in 1884[352].

– E.F. Kal', collegiate assessor[353]. His collection included manuscripts and archaeological (bones of men and animals, orna-ments, coins, stone beads, clay lamps, ceramics, fragments of arms and a silver cup with a silver bottom), numismatic and anthropolo-gical finds, bought in Khodjent, Tashkent, Samarkand, Yagnob, Kerki and Termez. After his death, in 1891, the collection was divi-ded between the Tashkent Museum (E.F. Kal' compiled the first catalogue of this collection in the 1880's[354]), the Archaeological Society, the Hermitage and the University of Saint-Petersburg. E.F. Kal' also made a catalogue of the oriental manuscripts of the Tashkent Public Library[355].

– N.A. Kashtalinsky, including "Bronze Age" antiques: "some rare specimens of bronze mirrors, faience figurines, various orna-ments for harness, a rare specimen of a bronze knife (*pernach*) and an axe, with which guards were armed", as well as Greek, Roman, Syrian, Arabian and Persian coins. The collector intended to dona-te his collection to the Archaeological Committee[356].

– A.V. Komarov, the first collector in Ashkhabad, whose house in 1890, to quote Count E.E. Ukhtomsky, was a "a real treasure of all possible local antiques". A special place was given to coins, which A.V. Komarov had started to collect while still in the

93. General A.V. Komarov, 1885.

Caucasus. In 1888 his collection comprised 18 golden, 206 silver and 463 copper Central Asian coins from the 8th century to modern times[357]. His collection of gems and Turkmen ethnographical objects was also quite remarkable[358].

– V.V. Krestovsky[359], who conducted excavations at Afrasiab in 1883, "in Timur's camp" near Samarkand, over the Dargom[360] and "in the Tashkent District near the village of Zerkend"[361]. During his excavations at Afrasiab he "collected 564 objects and compiled an album of 40 photographs, a copy of which he intended to send to the Archaeological Committee in Saint-Petersburg and another to the Moscow archaeological society"[362], but no trace of the albums has been discovered thus far. The collections themselves were divided up between the Tashkent Museum and the Archaeological Committee.

– N.F. Petrovsky, the Russian Consul in Kashgar during the period 1882-1904 (Buddhist Antiques, terracottas, a large collection of Hellenistic gems with inscriptions in Pehlevi; he offered many objects to the Hermitage, to the Asiatic Museum and to the Museum of the Russian Archaeological Society)[363].

– D.O. Petrov-Borzna (2,500 coins later classified by V.G. Tisenhausen and V.K. Savelyev, a ring bearing a Kufic inscription, carved stones with animal figures on them, signs of the zodiac, portraits of warriors, a head of an Indian woman, Arabian inscriptions, amulets and jewellery)[364].

– Prince Trubetskoy[365].

– A.A. Polovtsev[366].

Among these collections, especially that of Lieutenant General of the Engineers, I.T. Poslavsky[367], deserves special attention because of its typical fate and its importance. This collection is important together with a rich collection of decorative art, descriptions, plans, photographs and sketches of archaeological sites and architectural monuments (the ruins of Kunya-Paikend [1887], Khanabad-tepe [1907], Old Termez [1895], the Mausoleum of Hakim-al Termizi and the tower of "Gumbet-Kobuz"), and the drawings of rock paintings in Saimaly-Tash, discovered by N.G. Khludov and systematized for the first time by I.T. Poslavsky, who divided them into three categories. His collection also included archaeological finds[368].

The majority of these finds were collected in Termez, where Poslavsky conducted large-scale irrigation, engineering and construction work, connected with the deployment of the troops of the Termez military district in the western part of the Old Termez site[369].

Unique intaglios[370], bullae (off-prints of gems on clay), terracottas, carved alabaster stucco, ceramics, including a counterfeit Hellenistic vase with a relief, depicting crowded Bacchanal scenes, Stone Age tools, spherical and cone-shaped vases and coins constituted the core of the collection. Soon it was enriched with antiques from the collection of the military engineer, B.N. Kastalsky, who sold it to I.T. Poslavsky before going on to study at the Nikolsk Engineering Academy[371]. On his return to Central Asia B.N. Kastalsky made another collection, which was later divided among three museums: the Samarkand Museum (seals, gems, coins, ethnographical objects), the Hermitage (the Sasanid gems were published by A. Ja. Borisov and V.G. Lukonin) and the Moscow Museum of Oriental Cultures.

On the death of I.T. Poslavsky, in 1914, the Turkestanian Circle of Friends of Archaeology held a meeting in his memory, at which they decided, on L.A. Zimin's initiative, to publish a collection of archaeological papers by I.T. Poslavsky, including many descriptions of the objects in his collection[372]. Alas, the project was never carried out, and Poslavky's notes were lost.

After his death V.V. Bartold wrote that: "it would be good if Poslavsky's collection were transferred to some museum here or in

94. Some objects from the I.T. Poslavsky's collection, 1909.

Turkestan, but did not go abroad"[373].

The collection did not go abroad, but in 1917 it was nationalized. As a result, part of it was lost, and another part went to the Turkestan Oriental Institute where it was stored for a long time, together with other objects, in the archaeological and numismatical Cabinet, forming the core of the Institute's collection[374]. When the Turkestan Oriental Institute became part of the State University of Central Asia, namely its Oriental Faculty, the collection was given the status of the University Collection, but after the forced liquidation of the Oriental Faculty in 1931[375] the remains of the collection were brought to the Museum of Uzbekistan History[376]. In the words of O.Ju. Poslavskaya, the granddaughter of I.T. Poslavsky, "objects from grandfather's archaeological collection and the works of art collected by him" could later be seen in the Arts Museum of the Uzbekistan Republic[377].

For the 1890s one can mention the collections belonging to:

– L.S. Barszscewski[378], enriched during his numerous exploratory trips to the region and the excavations at Afrasiab, which was the largest site in the area.

According to D.I. Evarnitsky, it was based upon Sart Hafiz's collection, purchased in 1892 from his heirs by L.S. Barszscewski after his death[379]. The collection, offered for sale, in order to set up a museum in Samarkand, was described by D.I. Evarnitsky, who estimated that it would cost 1,800 roubles. D.E. Evarnitsky wrote, "Captain Barszscewski's collection consists, with a few exceptions, of antiques from the historical time BC and AD which belong to the so-called Greek Oriental epoch after Alexander the Great, but mainly to the Mongol era, especially to the epoch of Timur. In this respect Barszscewski's collection may be regarded as a demonstration of these two epochs as described by Professor N.I. Veselovsky of Saint-Petersburg University. The main collecting site was Afrasiab, the focal point of antiques in the Turkestan region, as well as other archaeological sites in eastern Bukhara. Barszscewski's present collection includes ceramic and metal objects, necklaces, glass, tools, penates, figurines and coins. Furthermore, the collection includes some pre-historic objects: two stone knives, one stone scraper, two exceptionally small celts, one bronze fibula or cloak-pin and one remarkably big bronze mirror. As for its size, Barszscewski's collection of antiques is one of the largest private collections in the region"[380].

But as there was no money in the state funds to buy the collection, part of it was bought by the Moscow merchant, N.I. Reshetnikov, who – in January 1896 – donated it to the Statistics Committee of the Samarkand Region to help set up the Samarkand Museum[381]. L.S. Barszscewski himself donated another part of the collection (according to M.E. Masson it was the least significant part[382]). According to N.Ja. Rostovtsev, the Archaeological Department of the Samarkand Museum "comprised his [Barszscewski's] collection". The same applied to the Palaeontological department[383]. The rest of the collection (one fifth) was bought for a well-known politician and businessman from Lyon, Lucien Mangini, by the French researcher and traveller, Jean Chaffanjon, for 240 roubles[384].

– V.L. Vyatkin, whose collection was based on finds made at Afrasiab. In the opinion of V.V. Bartold's, it was the most important archaeological collection in the region[385], museum collections being "negligible in comparison with it"[386].

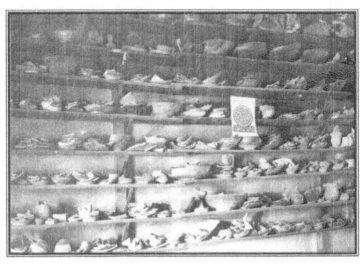

95. V.L. Vyatkin's collection, 1933.

– S.F. Nikolai (archaeological finds in the valley of the river Chirchik, donated to the Turkestanian Circle of Friends of Archaeology in 1907, later transferred to the Historical Museum in Tashkent[387]).

– Zampayev, who made his archaeological and numismatical collections in Termez[388].

– M. V. Stolyariov (archaeological finds from Afrasiab, including ceramics)[389].

The collections made in the first two decades of the 20th century were those of N.S. Lykoshin, R. Pumpelly (archaeological objects collected in Old Merv and Anau), G.A. Shamsutdinov (archaeological and numismatic collections) and J.-A. Castagné, then a Russian citizen[390].

96. V.L. Vyatkin's collection in his cellar, 1933.

97. Committee for the acquisition of V.L. Vyatkin's collection, 1933.

The collection of J.-A. Castagné, regarded by experts as one of the best in Turkestan, was highly appreciated by V.V. Bartold, who wrote that it was "the result of numerous trips and journeys and is stored in perfect order, with a precise note on the origin of every object"[391]. Having taken over the collection, while still in Orenburg, J.-A. Castagné added things to it which he had bought or discovered while on his own archaeological excavations. Most of the collection consisted of the material picked up on the surface: 12th- 20th century ceramics, fragments of glass vessels, copperware, terracotta figurines, and adornments made of stone, copper and glass. In addition to the archaeological collection J.-A. Castagné possessed a rich ethnographical collection (in particular, he bought part of A.I. Dobrosmyslov's collection after his death. In 1916 he donated 23 objects belonging to it to the Orenburg Museum: jewellery, hunting objects and other everyday objects[392]) and a collection

98. Stone babas from the Kazakh Steppe, by J.-A. Castagné.

of books on the history, archaeology and ethnography of Turkestan, many of which he donated to the Turkestanian Circle of Friends of Archaeology and the Turkestan Department of the Imperial Russian Geographical Society[393]. In 1920 over 500 objects, registered in 23 catalogues of collections, were sold to the Turkestan Popular Museum. Archaeological objects which had no connection whatsoever with Turkestan, as well as ethnographical collections, were given to the museum, gratis. G.N. Chabrov mentions that part of this collection was sold to the Hermitage, but thus far no documents have been found proving this. Likewise, the part of the collection which J.-A. Castagné took to France, remains unidentified[394].

Numismatical collections, ranking fourth, were not so directly connected with the development of Archaeology in Central Asia: rather than buying directly from private collections, the main source of new acquisitions was the market, where coins were brought to indirectly. However, their development is very much like that of the archaeological collections[395], of which coins constitute an essential part. There are some collections, though, in which only numismatic material is attested to by our evidence (without archaeological objects). In 1850s such were the collections of Velyaminov-Zernov[396] and Grigoryev, whose collection was partly made up of the coin hoard found near Khodjent[397]; in 1860s: the collections of Major-General Abramov and General Golovachev[398]; in 1870s-1880s: Fadeev, Grombchevsky, Gelmann, Linevich, Trofimov.

Architectural details, as well as coins, were often included in archaeological collections[399].
    Among the architectural objects, the objects most popular with collectors were tiles: nearly every traveller was eager to take a piece of sparkling majolica home with him as a souvenir. Their popularity was encouraged by the widespread European idea that architecture was the only field of art in which the creativity of oriental people was fully understood, by the deplorable state of the monuments – which by the mid-19th century had turned into romantic ruins – and by the low price this kind of object fetched. For 5 roubles it was possible to buy several ceramic objects. In spite of the official prohibitions, the "curators", including clergy, were

willing to sell any of
the details of a monu-
ment and to help take
them down from the
walls of the monu-
ments[400]. Samarkand
and Bukhara were
main focal points in
this respect. Often the
details in question
were not just frag-
ments, but entire
panels, as for example
in the case of the
mosaic portal panel
from the Mausoleum
Gur-Emir, taken down
from the monument in
1905 and shipped to

99. General A.K. Abramov, by P. Borel, 1870s.

Constantinople, where in 1906 it was bought by the Kaiser
Friedrich Museum in Berlin, and later, after long diplomatic nego-
tiations, purchased by the Russian Government[401].

Marble facing shared much the same destiny: "Big pieces with
inscriptions upon them were broken off from the corners of two
marble gravestones of Bureida and Hakam near Old Merv and take
away from Asia by the Englishmen who were there in the summer
of 1893", according to a letter sent to the Imperial Archaeological
Committee on 2nd February, 1895[402].

But storing huge architectural details at home was rather incon-
venient, and tile collections were usually given to museums or were
made on their request. However, there were some exceptions to this
rule. In the 1900s, in Samarkand, the attention of travellers was
often drawn to a private house, whose façade was tiled with ceramic fragments "borrowed" from famous monuments[403]. In Russian
Turkestan it was not uncommon to re-use old bricks and facing
material for new buildings (bricks from the ruins of Djankent were
used for the construction of Kazalinsk; bricks taken from the ruins
of a burial mound were utilized for construction works in Chinaz,

etc.). This practice did not affect the scientists: N.N. Veselovsky, representing the Russian Imperial Archaeological Committee, agreed to authorize the "native Turdybaev" to re-use bricks from the Ishrat-Khana Mausoleum for the construction of Hujr. His only precaution was to allocate S.M. Dudin the task of taking photographs and drawings, and collecting mosaics (these were bought for ten roubles)[404].

Concern for the safety of architectural details is very often expressed in the works of researchers and travellers of the late 19th century. Thus, S.M. Dudin even suggested taking apart the decorative facing of Bibi-Khanym and Ishrat-khana and transferring it to the Hermitage, which he thought would be more sensible than leaving it at their place where it would be at the mercy of "natural des-

100. Shah-i Zindah in Samarkand.
Anonymous photographer.

truction and plundering by all sorts traders of antiques"[405] (the method of transferral was used by French explorers in the Near East and by German explorers in Chinese Turkestan, e.g. Albert Grünwedel and Albert von Le Coq).

The decline in collecting architectural details was, on the one hand, due to the fact that private collecting was supplanted in this field by planned collecting for museums, and, on the other hand, to the measures taken by the state and learned societies in order to preserve the monuments (in 1913-1914 the Russian Committee for the Study of Central and Eastern Asia assumed responsibility for preserving monuments; in 1914 the Duma discussed the project entailing annual allocations for preserving the most important Central Asian monuments; a programme for the preservation of historical monuments was still carried out by the Turkestanian Circle of Friends of Archaeology).

During this period architectural details are to be seen in the Russian collections of A.L. Kun (in 1871 he sent 15 cases of architectural fragments to the museum of the Archaeological Committee in Saint-Petersburg, from where the collection was sent "to the palace of Her Imperial Highness, the Grand Duchess Maria Nikolayevna, president of the Society for the Promotion of Arts and President of the Academy of Arts, where it became one of the best pieces in the Museum of Industry organized there"[406], and was later transferred to the Museum

101. Fragments of enamelled bricks and of marble from Samarkand in Ch.-E. Ujfalvy's collection, 1880s.

of the Society for the Promotion of the Arts); of S.M. Dudin (who made it for the Russian Museum); D.M. Rezvoi (objects from Kunya-Urgench); A.A. Bobrinsky (architectural details of traditional Tajik houses from Darvaz); A.A. Polovtsev, who sent specimens of Central Asian tiles and carved stucco from the 14th and 15th centuries to the Museum of Baron Stiglitz' Art School; of the Frenchman, H.R. d'Allemagne, who sent – to the address of the Minister of Public Instruction – 55 kilograms of architectural ceramics (1898, 1907), and of Ch.-E. Ujfalvy.

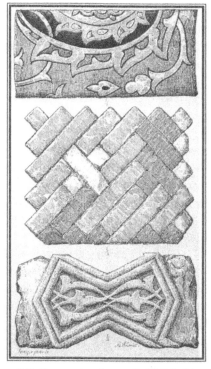

102. Fragments of enamelled bricks from Samarkand and Djankend (region of Aral Lake) in Ch.-E. Ujfalvy's collection, 1880s.

Anthropological objects were also popular with the collectors. Proceeding from the then popular idea that "the Nestorians appear to be an unknown race which ceased to exist", many West European travellers collected gravestones and skulls from Nestorian cemeteries. In 1890-1891 E. Blanc made a collection of Nestorian skulls in Tokmak, Peshkek (Peshpek, Bishkek) and Verny (Vernij, Vierny, Alma-Ata). Together, the Russian researcher, N.N. Pantusov, and the engineer, P.V. Gurde, J. Chaffanjon, made a collection of 20 Nestorian skulls and gravestones "decorated with a Greek Cross and inscribed in Syriac" near Alma-Ata, Bishkek and Tokmak. In 1912, E. Hindamian brought – from Samarkand to Paris – 13 Nestorian stelae from the 13th and 14th centuries, found in Semirechye by Poyarkov and Andreyev, which he donated, together with other objects (inscribed tablets and vases) to the Guimet Museum in Paris (later they were divided up between the Guimet Museum in Lyon [6 stelae, later transferred to the Arts Museum of Lyon] and the Louvre)[407].

Manuscript collections[408] came into being in accordance with other laws. The tradition of collecting manuscripts, unlike archaeological objects, was widespread in the East. The best known court libraries were: the library of the Samanid dynasty in Bukhara (819-999) later destroyed by a fire; that of the Mamunids (the second dynasty of Khwarezm-Shahs) (992-1017); of the Timurid dynasty in Samarkand (14th-15th century); of the Sheibanids in Bukhara (1500-1598), and later the library of the Ashtarkhanid dynasty (17th- 18th century).

By the 19th century the largest collections of manuscripts were concentrated in the libraries of the Central Asian rulers, clergy, high-ranking officials and in medreses and mosques, thus being accessible to the public. The Emir of Bukhara owned a large library, comprising 50,000 volumes. In 1908 A.N. Samoilovich saw two of the Emir's libraries: one in the Arka khan's official residence in the citadel, and the other in his palace at Taza Bag, where – from 1874 onwards – the khan's lithography workshop was located. A precise description of the collection was not made during this period, and even five years later Emir Muhammad Alim-Khân did not allow A.Z. Validi to make a catalogue of the royal libraries in Bukhara and Karmina on his research trip to Bukhara (1913-1915)[409]. V.V. Bartold, A.Z. Validi and A. Fitrat report that other important collections of manuscripts and books were in the possession of the inhabitants of Turkestan[410]: in Tashkent[411], Bukhara[412], Kokand[413], Samarkand[414], Shahr-i Sabz[415] and Karshi[416].

It was not uncommon for the owners of large libraries to be booksellers, at one and the same time, as was the case with the tradesman, Mullâ Najm Al-dîn of Karshi, who owned bookstalls in Karshi and in Bukhara, with thousands of volumes in all of the languages of the region[417], or "the *aksakal* of the Bukhara booksellers" Mullâ Sheref Al-dîn. A big bookstall on the Voskresensky Market in Tashkent belonged to a Jewish trader, Leibe Schwartz, in the period 1870-1890, and was renamed the "Bookinist" by his son Abram

Leibovich Kirsner in 1892[418]. The main tasks of the scholars consisted in discovering, systematizing and studying the collections, which already existed in Turkestan.

The Turkestan authorities also made attempts to register all of the important private collections and to buy them, after the owners' death, for the Tashkent Public Library[419], thus saving them from destruction or from being divided up among the heirs because of the

103. Ishan Khodja, judge (kazy) of Samarkand, 1871-1872. Anonymous photographer.

Shariat laws of inheritance (sometimes old manuscripts were sold "dirt cheap to bookbinders who used them as cardboard for binding"[420]).

On the other hand, though manuscripts were associated with the idea of wealth, for a normal European, a manuscript collection was a far cry from the luxury and prestige attached to carpet collections. Consequently, the circle of Russians and foreigners interested in these kinds of "antiques" was confined to orientalists, who made collections not for themselves, but in the name of "scholarship". Therefore, the manuscripts collected by them usually went to museums and libraries[421]. One of the earliest examples was N.V. Khanykov's collection, made in the 1840s, which was partly incorporated into the Asiatic Museum in the 1850s and partly (161 manuscripts) purchased by Saint-Petersburg Public Library in 1864[422].

It must be noted that the tradition of collecting oriental manuscripts in Russia dates back to the age of Peter the Great, when they were concentrated in his "cabinet of curiosities" (the first descriptions of the Kunstkamera collections were published in the 1730s). Afterwards, the Oriental Cabinet was based at the Kunstkamera, which was later called the "Asiatic Museum" and by the middle of the 18th century it possessed some 4,000 oriental manuscripts, including a number of Central Asian manuscripts, to which the pri-

104. Manuscript. Firman of Bukhara.

vate collections of N.V. Khanykov, P.I. Lerch and others were added[423].

The collecting of oriental manuscripts was further stimulated by the development of orientalist training (Lazarev Institute in Moscow, 1815-1816; Educational Department of Oriental Languages at the Ministry of Foreign Affairs, 1823; Chairs of Oriental languages at the Universities of Kharkov (1804), Kazan (1804), Moscow (1804) and Saint-Petersburg (1816); Russian Committee for the study of Central and Oriental Asia, 1903).

At this time, collecting was deliberate and planned. In 1834 Academician Ch.D. Fren, the first director of the Asiatic Museum, prepared *A Chronological list of 100 Works, Mostly Historical and Geographical, in Arabic, Persian and Turkish, Missing for the Most Part in European Libraries, where Originals or Reliable Copies Should Be Found for the Sake of Scholarship, Especially by Those Who Come to Be in the East.* For many travellers it served as a kind of guide to buying manuscripts (later it was re-edited to include more than 200 items). On his journey, in 1858, P.I. Lerch distributed this list of *desiderata* "in Khiva and Bukhara among those who could help to buy rare books"[424].

A special page in the history of the collecting of manuscripts was written by those attempting to find Timur's library, both imperial officials and orientalists (A. Vambery, A.L. Kun, D.N. Logofet and others)[425]. According to some scholars, the only manuscript found, which might have belonged to Timur's library, was the famous Osman's Koran. Sergent Serov, who collected information on antiques on the orders of the Head of the Zarafshan Region, Major-General Abramov, reported in 1869 that the Koran was in the Samarkand mosque of Khodja-Ahrar. Bought by Abramov for 125 roubles, the Koran was transferred by von Kaufmann in 1876 to the Public Library of Saint-Petersburg. Today the Central Administrative Board of the Moslems of Uzbekistan has it in safe keeping in Tashkent[426].

The most well-known collections of Russian manuscripts are associated with the following names: V.V. Bartold[427], V.V. Velyaminov-Zernov, N.I. Veselovsky, V.L. Vyatkin[428], M.V. Gavrilov, D.M. Gramenitsky[429], V.V. Grigoryev, K.G. Saleman, V.A. Ivanov[430], V.I. Ignatyev, A.D. Kalmykov, K.P. von Kaufmann, E.F. Kal'[431], A.L. Kun[432], V.P. Nalivkin, P.I. Lerch[433], Ja.Ja. Lutsh[434], F.F. Popelov, D.O. Petrov-Borzna, N.F. Petrovsky[435], N.N. Pantusov, V.V. Radlov, A.N. Samoilovich[436], A.A. Semenov[437] and N.V. Khanykov, although manuscripts were often to be found in the collections of those interested in the history of

105. Osman's Koran and Soviet scientists, 1925.

Turkestan[438].

Among the western collectors, noteworthy collections were made by Elkan Nathan Adler[439], Silvestre de Sasy, E. Quatremère, P. Aubry, J.-A. Decourdemanche, E. Blanc[440].

The following collections stood apart by virtue of their unusual character:

1 – *collections of the working archives of local artisans (usto)*[441], consisting of specimens of local decorative art, work drawings, drafts, detailed descriptions of techniques and technology handed down from one generation to the next, together with the special knowledge of their craft. An interesting collection of this nature was made by M.S. Andreyev, who was in charge of decoration work in the house of A.A. Polovtsev (the house had to be decorated in the "national" style)[442]. Collections of specimens of traditional decoration in the form of albums and tables (Mîrzâ Barat Kasymov[443], S.M. Dudin, G.A. Pankratyev, N.E. Simakov[444], A. Voronina-Utkina[445], A.P. Mataftin[446], A. Astafyev[447], N.N. Shcherbina-Kramarenko, G.G. Shmidt[448], B.N. Litvinov[449]) are closely connected with this category.

2 – collections of *personal sketches and drawings* done in Turkestan by professional artists (the painters V.V. Vereshchagin, S.M. Dudin, L.I. Bure, L.E. Dmitriev-Kavkazsky, R.Ch. Sommer, N.N. Karazin, A. Pepin, J. Laurens, B. Zaleski, the sculptor P.P. Kamensky[450] and others) and by amateurs (scholars P.I. Lerch, O.A. and A.P. Fedchenko, O. Olufsen; military men – M. Alikhanov-Avarsky, A. Astafyev, D.M. Rezvoi, K. Dickhof[451] and medical men)[452]. Being typical examples of the ethnographical branch of Russian Oriental Studies, these collections, which are now on display in museums[453] or in private and state archives, require a different kind of analysis, going far beyond the limits of the history of collections[454].

3 – collections of *photographs*[455] of Central Asian architectural monuments, objects of decorative art and ethnic types. The largest Russian collections were: A.L. Kun's *Turkestanian Album* (1873-1874)[456], photographs taken by L.S. Barszscewski, Bykovsky, S.M. Dudin[457], B.N. Kastalsky, N.N. Nekhoroshev, S.F. Nikolai, G.A. Pankratyev, N.N. Pantusov, N.F. Petrovsky[458], A.A. Polovtsev,

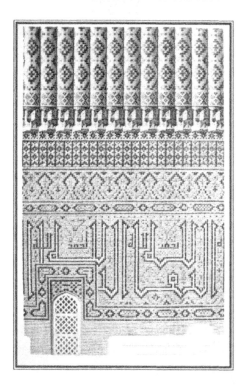

106. Cupola of the Gur Emir at Samarkand, by A. Shcherbina-Kramarenko, 1895-1899.

107. Inner niche in the North of the Gur Emir, by A. Shcherbina-Kramarenko, 1895-1899.

S.M. Prokudin-Gorsky and others[459].

Among the photographs taken by Europeans, of particular interest are those by R. Bonaparte, S. Borghese, L. Blot, J. Brocherel, Henri de Bouillane de Lacoste, G. Capus, J. Chaffanjon, H. Dauvergne, E. Gallois, L. Gay, M. Hordet, G. Durant, H. Krafft, P. Labbé, A. de La Baume Pluvinel, P. Lessar, E. Maillart, J. Martin, H. Moser, P. Nadar, O. Olufsen, E. de Poncins, W. Rickmer Rickmers, A. Roger-Viollet, S. Salm, Ch.-Eu. Ujfalvy, which are mostly unpublished[460].

Later on, when many monuments were partly or completely destroyed or even lost, materials from these collections became very precious and were sometimes the only source available for the study of the history of Central Asian art (above all, of architecture).

* * *

In conclusion we can say with certainty that the phenomenon of collecting in Turkestan and especially the popularization of the collections by their owners in the second half of the 19th century and in the early 20th century drew the attention of scholars from all over the world to the culture and history of Central Asia, thus opening up new prospects for the study of practically unknown and unique material, sparking off long scholarly discussions and arousing public interest in the Central Asian region[461].

Appendix

List of the Turkestanian (T), Russian (R), and International (I) Exhibitions of the 2nd Half of the 19th and Early 20th Century in which Private Collections of Russian Turkestan have been presented (See also note 203)

1867 (T) – Exhibition of various objects made by local artisans (Tashkent); was organized by the Head of the Khodjent District Colonel A.A. Kushakevich.

1867 (R) – Ethnographical Russian Exhibition (Moscow); was organized at Moscow University by the Society of Friends of Natural History, Anthropology and Ethnography, for the first time in Russia, together with a Turkestanian Department. Collections belonging to the following people have been exhibited: O.A. Fedchenko, V.F. Oshanin collected in Tashkent), General Kolpakovsky (compiled in Kirghizia), Ju.D. Juzhakov (models of traditional houses), and the album of drawings "Great Horde and Savage Kirghiz" by the artist N.M. Kosharov (S.M. Abramzon, "Etnograficheskij al'bom khudozhnika N.M. Kosharova [Ethnographic Album of the Painter N.M. Kosharov]", *Sbornik Muzeja antropologii i etnografii AN SSSR* [Collected Papers of the Museum of Anthropology and Ethnography, the Academy of Sciences of the USSR], t. 14, Leningrad, 1953, p. 147-192). All objects were gathered over a period of two years by the Heads of the Khodjent District - Colonel A.A. Kushakevich and Colonel Rondatti, and were sent by General M.G. Chernyaev (*Ukazatel' Russkoj etnograficheskoj vystavki, ustroennoj Obshchestvom ljubitelej estestvoznanija, sostojashchem pri Imperatorskom Moskovskom Universitete* [Catalogue of the Russian Ethnographical Exhibition, organized by the Society of the Friends of Natural History at Moscow Imperial University], Moscow, 1867; V.V. Stasov, "Nasha sredneaziatskaja vystavka i ee kritiki [Our Central Asian Exhibition and its critics]", *Sobranie sochinenij* [Collected Works], Saint-Petersburg, 1894, p. 935, 946). After this exhibition almost all of the Central Asian collections were donated to the Dashkova Museum (V.O. Miller, *Sistematicheskoe opisanie kollekcij Dashkovskogo Etnograficheskogo muzeja* [A Systematic Description of the Dashkova Ethnographic Museum], Moscow, 1887, p. IX-X).

1869 (R) – Exhibition "Proizvedenij kraja [Creations of the Country]" (Saint-Petersburg). Same participants as in previous exhibition.

1870 (R) – All-Russian Manufactures Exhibition (Saint-Petersburg). 2,000 objects made by the artisans of Tashkent, Khodjent and Ura-Tyube.

1870 (T) – Industrial Exhibition (Tashkent). Collections of traditional artists (ceramics, carved wood).

1872 (R) – All-Russian Polytechnical Exhibition (was organized by the Society of the Friends of Natural History, Anthropology and Ethnography, Moscow). The face of the Turkestan Pavilion (which was subdivided into seven sections) was decorated with paintings by O.A. Fedchenko and D.L. Ivanov imitating the face of the Shir-Dor Medressah at Samarkand. The ethnographic collections of O.A. Fedchenko were exhibited and copies of watercolours by A.K. Savrasov and P.A. Niseven; the collections of D.L. Ivanov, N.A. Kryzhanovsky, L.F. Ballyuzek, Colonel Ch. Valikhanov, G.A. Kolpakovsky (religious, ethnographical objects, and arms made in the Kuldja District of China), D.L. Ivanov (hunting objects), General N.N. Golovachev (coins). The catalogue has been prepared by M.I. Brodovsky, I.I. Krause, A.P. and O.A. Fedchenko (*Katalog Turkestanskogo otdela Vserossijskoj Politekhnicheskoj vystavki 1872 g.* [Catalogue of the Turkestanian Section of the All-Russian Polytechnical Exhibition of 1872], Moscow, 1872). After the exhibition some objects were donated to the Dashkova Museum and, after 1917, transferred to the Moscow Museum of the Peoples of the USSR.

1873 (I) – Exhibition in Vienna (dir. D.L. Ivanov). Some of the objects were the same as those on display in the exhibition of 1872.

1876 (I) – Exhibition during the III[rd.] International Congress of Orientalists in Saint-Petersburg (organized by P.I. Lerch)

1877 (R) – Exhibition at the IVth Archaeological Congress in Kazan. A.L. Kun's collections.

1878 (T) – Turkestanian Agricultural Exhibition (Tashkent). Mîrzâ Bukhari's collection (gold medal received for the collection of silk products).

1878 (I) – International Exhibition in Paris, with Ujfalvy's collection.

1879 (R) – Anthropological Exhibition (Moscow). Turkestan was represented by M.M. Virsky's archaeological collection.

1882 (R) – All-Russian Artistic and Industrial Exhibition (Moscow). Various objects made by local artisans (silks, fabrics, metalwork, jewellery, arms).

1886 (T) – Turkestan Exhibition of Agricultural and Industrial Objects (Tashkent). Mîrzâ Bukhari's collections.

1886 (T) – Turkestan Artistic and Industrial Exhibition (Tashkent). Department with various objects made by local artisans. Mîrzâ Barat Kasymov's collection of architectural decoration and tombstones from Samarkand.

1887 (R) – Agricultural Exhibition (Kharkov). Mîrzâ Bukhari's collection (gold medal for the collection of silk and fabrics).

1887 (R) – Exhibition of Central Asian manuscripts 15th-17th centuries in the Department of manuscripts of the Saint-Petersburg Public Library (*Imperatorskaja publichnaja biblioteka za 100 let* [*op. cit.* note 422]).

1888 (T) – Artistic Exhibition from N.K. Romanov's collection: 35 specimens of European and Russian art, e.g. Veronese, Annibal Carrach, Teniers, Jacob Ruysdaël, Natiet, Sverchkov, Myasoedov, Jakobi, Gay, Semiradsky, Shilder, Levitsky, Lampi, and others; objects from the Khivan expedition (Tashkent).

1888 (I) – International Exhibition in Copenhagen. Plates from N.S. Simakov's Album of Ornaments (N. Simakov, *op. cit.* [note 444]).

1890 (T) – Exhibition for the 25th Jubilee of the Conquest of Tashkent "Turkestan Artistic and Industrial Exhibition" (Tashkent). Akram Askarov's Archaeological and Numismatical collections were presented in a special pavilion, which he constructed by himself. Mîrzâ Bukhari's numismatic collection. Artisans' productions.

1891 (R) – Exhibition on Central Asia in Moscow (*Katalog sredneaziatskoj vystavke v Moskve* [Catalogue of Central Asia], Moscow, 1891).

1892 (T) – Exhibition of hunting objects (D.L. Ivanov's collection of hunting objects belonging to local inhabitants ?).

1893 – Universal exhibition in Honour of Columbus at Chicago, where the Turkestan's pavilion imitated the Bukharan Emir's country residence of Shir-Budan. Paintings by R. Sommer and P.Ja. Pesetsky (*Vsemirnaja Kolumbova Vystavka 1893 goda v Chikago. Ukazatel' Russkogo Otdela* [Universal Exhibition in Honour of Columbus 1893 at Chicago. Guide to the Russian Department], Saint-Petersburg, 1893, p.209, 453).

1893-1894 (R) – Humanitarian Exhibition at the Hermitage. With the collection of Grand-Duke Nicolas II Romanov's gifts, organized by General-Adjudant K.N. Pos'et and I.A. Sytenko; catalogue published by E.E. Ukhtomsky.

1896 (R) – All-Russian Industrial and Artisans Exhibition at Nijni-Novgorod, with a Turkestan's pavilion in Mauritanian style by the architect A.I. Pomerantsev. Bukharan Emir's collection (*Vserossijskaja khudojstvenno-promyshlennaja vystavka 1896 goda v Nijnem Novgorode* [All-Russian Industrial and Artisans Exhibition 1896 at Nijni-Novgorod], Saint-Petersburg, 1896).

1897 (I) – Islamic Exhibition in Stockholm. Fredrik Martin's collections.

1899 (T) – First Turkestanian Photographic Exhibition (Tashkent). Collections of photographs by L.S. Barszscewski, Bykovsky, B.N. Kastalsky, N.N. Nekhoroshev, S.F. Nikolai, G.A. Pankratyev, A.A. Polovtsev.

1900 (I) – Paris Universal Exhibition. K.A. Korovin decorated the Central Asian Pavilion with huge panels framed with carpets. Contained the G.A. Arendorenko's carpet collection; the Bukharan Emir's collection, which was permanently surveyed by two of the emir's representatives dressed in rich clothes (more than 300 objects: clothes with golden embroidery, fabrics, jewels, artistic metalwork, arms); the Khivan Khan's collections and collections of the Tashkent, Samarkand, Ferghana and Ashkhabad Museums (*Parizhskaja vsemirnaja vystavka 1900 goda. Obshchij obzor vystavki* [Paris 1900 Universal Exhibition. General Survey of the Exhibition], Saint-Petersburg, 1901; *Vsemirnaja parizhskaja vystavka v illustracijakh i opisanijakh* [Paris Universal Exhibition through illustrations and descriptions], ed. M.A. Orlov, 1900; *Turkestanskie Vedomosti* [The Turkestanian News], 1899, N° 50, 97).

1902 (R) – All-Russian Industrial and Artisans Exhibition (Saint-Petersburg in the Tauric Palace). Carpet collections of A.A. Bogolyubov, A.A. Falkersam, Bukharan Emir.

1902 (R) – First International Exhibition of historical and modern costumes and their accessories (Saint-Petersburg). Bukharan Emir's clothes collection.

1903 (R) – First International Artistic and Industrial Exhibition of stone and metal objects (Saint-Petersburg). Bukharan Emir's collection.

1903 (R) – International Scientific and Artistic Exhibition "World of childhood" (Saint-Petersburg). Toys and children's clothes from Bukhara (32 exhibits).

1904 (R) – Great Historical Exhibition of Works of Art organized at the Museum of Baron Stiglitz' Art School (Saint-Petersburg). N.F. Burdukov's, A.A. Falkersam's and Bukharan Emir's carpet collections.

1904 (I) – International Exhibition in Saint-Louis (USA). Bukharan Emir's collections (128 exhibit).

1905 (I) – International Exhibition at Liege (Lüttich, Belgium). Bukharan Emir's collections.

1906 (I) – Exhibition in Milan. Bukharan Emir's collections.

1907 (I) – Exhibition in Bordeaux. Bukharan Emir's collections.

1907 (R) – All-Russian Artisans Exhibition (Saint-Petersburg). Collections from the Turkestan museums; Bukharan Emir's collection (the same that had been exhibited in Milan and Bordeaux: silk and linen fabrics, carpets, arms, golden embroidered clothes, jewels, artistic metalwork).

1909 (T) – Turkestan's Industrial, Agricultural, Scientific and Artistic Exhibition (Tashkent). S.M. Dukhovskoy's and Mishchenko's arms collections; arms and metal-vessels collection from Kokand (had probably been made by A. Kun during the conquest of Kokand in 1876). The map with indications of the diffusion of carpet production was presented in the Trans-Caspian District section; I.T. Poslavsky's gems collection; G.A. Shamsutdinov's archaeological and numismatic collections; paintings about Turkestan by S.P. Yudin, N. Razanov, M.O. Mikeshin and others amateurs presented in the Military Section (*Katalog voennogo otdelenija Turkestanskoj promyshlennoj, sel'sko-khozja-jstvennoj, nauchnoj i khudozhestvennoj vystavki, 1909 god* [Catalogue of the Military Department of the Turkestanian Industrial, Agricultural, Scientific and Art Exhibition, 1909], Tashkent, 1909; *Katalog-putevoditel' Turkestanskoj XXV-letnej Jubilejnoj promyshlennoj, sel'sko-khozjajstvennoj, nauchnoj i khu-dozhestvonnoj vystavki* [Guide-Catalogue of the Turkestanian 25th jubilee of the Industrial, Agricultural, Scientific and Artistic Exhibition], Tashkent, 1909).

1910 (I) – Great Islamic Exhibition (Munich). Art objects from the Hermitage and the Armoury of the Kremlin; Fredrik Martin's collection.

1911 (I) – Exhibition in Turin.

1911 (T) – First Turkestan Exhibition of paintings (Tashkent). It was organized by the Pushkin Society (paintings, photographs, carpets, furniture, handicrafts, archaeological objects, coins) (*Turkestanskie Vedomosti* [The Turkestanian News], 1911, N° 55, 62).

1911 (T) – First Carpet Exhibition of Ashkhabad (150 items).

1912-1913 (T) – Carpet Exhibition at Tashkent, Merv and Krasnovodsk. It was organized by the Head of Krasnovodsk Department Karninsky.

1913 (R) – Second All-Russian Handicraft Exhibition (Saint-Petersburg). Items from Museum collections or Turkestanian merchants (carpets, embroidery, jewellery).

1913 (T) – Carpet Exhibition of Ashkhabad.

1914 (I) – Trans-Caspian Region's Carpet Exhibition in Berlin.

1914 (I) – Trans-Caspian Region's Carpet Exhibition in London.

1915 (T) – Exhibition organized by the Society of Fine Arts and Handicrafts in the house of the merchant, Zaho (N.K. Romanov's collection, local artists).

1915 (T) – Itinerant Exhibition in the stations along the Trans-Caspian railway organized by the amateur artist Vlasov (paintings, sculptures, insect collections, models of animals, arms, coins, archaeological objects) (*Turkestanskie Vedomosti* [The Turkestanian News], 1915, N° 96, 152).

Notes

[1] *L'Anticomanie: la collection d'antiquités aux 18e et 19e siècles*, [colloque international, Montpellier-Lattes, 9-12 juin 1988], textes rassemblés par A.-F. Laurens et Kr. Pomian, Paris, Ed. de l'EHESS, Collection Civilisations et sociétés, 86, 1992, p. 18.

[2] Translation by S. Stepantsov (Moscow) and Mrs. D. Le Guillou (Halle).

[3] The term "Central Asia" is used here in a narrower sense than in western research works and refers to Russian scholarly usage. It applies to the territory of Russian Turkestan in the 19th and early 20th century, including the former Soviet republics of Uzbekistan, Tajikistan, Turkmenistan and Kirghizstan (with the exception of Kazakhstan, which at the time of Russian colonization was under the control of the governor-general of Orenburg). The region in question was sometimes called Transoxiana (a Hellenizing calque of the Arabian term Maveronnahr) or Western Turkestan.

[4] In Russian and Soviet research literature, the history of private collections was partly dealt with in the works of M.E. Masson, G.A. Pugachenkova, N.S. Sadykova, V.G. Shkoda, A.A. Semenov, V.V. Stasov, O.A. Sukhareva and others. The most important contributions were those of G.N. Chabrov and B.V. Lunin. The problem of the numismatics collections has been lastly treated by A. Naymark.

[5] See, for example: M. Rheims, *Les Collectionneurs: De la Curiosité, de la beauté, du goût, de la mode, et de la spéculation*, Edition Ramsay, Paris, 1981, 457 p.; Kr. Pomian, *Collectionneurs, amateurs et curieux, Paris, Venise, XVIe-XVIIIe siècle*, [Paris], Gallimard, Collection Bibliothèque des histoires, 1987, 364 p.; *Le commerce de l'art, de la Renaissance à nos jours*, sous la dir. de L. Bertrand Dorleac; introd. de Kr. Pomian, Besançon, La Manufacture, 1992, 357 p.; *L'anticomanie, op.cit.* (note 2), 351 p.; A. Schnapper, *Collections et collectionneurs dans la France du XVIIe siècle*, Paris, Flammarion, 1988-1994, 2 v.; W. Muensterberger, *Le collectionneur: anatomie d'une passion*, Paris, Edition Payot & Rivages, 1996, 326 p.

[6] E.g., the drawing by K. Meinshausen, illustrating the botanical collection of A.I. Schrenck, made in Djungaria in 1840-1841 (Saint-

Petersburg Botanical Gardens) and numerous illustrations in *Turkestanskij sbornik sochinenij i statej, otnosjashchikhsja do Srednej Azii voobshche i Turkestanskogo kraja v osobennosti, sostavlennyj po porucheniju Turkestanskogo general-gubernatora K.P. Kaufmana, V.I. Mezhovym* [A Turkestanian collection of papers and studies devoted to Central Asia in general and to Turkestan in particular, edited by V.I. Mezhov on the orders of the Governor-General of Turkestan, K.P. Kaufmann], 1867-1916.

[7] A rare case of the works of western art being present in a Turkestanian collection is that of the collection of Grand Duke N.K. Romanov, which included Russian and Western European paintings. See: *Turkestanskie Vedomosti* [The Turkestanian News], 1888, N° 2, Appendix: *Katalog kartin i dostorpimechatel'nostej iz kollekcii ego imperatorskogo velichestva velikogo knjazja Nikolaja Konstantinovicha* [The Catalogue of Paintings and Curiosities in the Collection of His Imperial Highness, the Grand Duke Nikolai Konstantinovich].

[8] Meanwhile, some important collections were made in Soviet Central Asia. Thus, the large collections of D. Biryukov, B. Golender, A. Ivkov, E. Fogel', B. Knopov, V. Kucherov, Markov, Otboyev, Turchinsky, and others came into being during the last decades of Soviet rule. Modern Central Asian collections are dealt with in a work by I. Bogoslovskaya, on the basis of collections made in the USA. * See also *Addenda, infra*, p. 205.

[9] Among the nationalized collections were those of the White House of the governor-general of Turkestan, of B.N. Kastalsky, N.S. Lykoshin, N.A. Polovtsev, I.T. Poslavsky, N.K. Romanov, V.L. Vyatkin and others.

[10] Al. Kammerer, *La découverte de la Chine par les Portugais au XVIe siècle et la cartographie des portulans*, avec des notes de toponymie chinoise, par Paul Pelliot, Leiden, E.J. Brill, 1944, IX-260 p.

[11] From the 16th century until the Russian conquest of Central Asia, the Transoxianian region was divided up among many unstable state units, which by the beginning of the 19th century formed three durable Uzbekian Khanates: the Khivan Khanate (the Kungrad dynasty), the Kokand Khanate (the Ming dynasty) and the Bukhara Emirate (the Astrakhanids, later the Mangits dynasty), surrounded by a moving nomadic periphery. The present day Kazakh steppes were divided up among three nomadic tribal groups: the Great, the Middle and the Little Hordes (Jouzes).

[12] In 1501 the Safavids dynasty took over power in Iran, turning the country, where the Sunnites had hitherto prevailed, into a state of the

Shi'ites, who were ideologically opposed to the orthodox Sunnite Uzbekian Khanates.

[13] H. Carrère D'Encausse, "Les routes commerciales de l'Asie centrale et les tentatives de reconquête d'Astrakhan d'après les registres des "Affaires importantes "des Archives ottomanes", *Cahiers du monde russe et soviétique*, 1970, XI, p. 416-417; N. Steensgaard, *The Asian trade revolution of the seventeenth century: the East India companies and the decline of the caravan trade*, Chicago, University of Chicago Press, [1974], 441 p.; M. Rossabi, "The Decline of the Central Asian Caravan Trade", *in* J.D. Tracy, *The Rise of Merchant Empires,* Cambridge, 1990, p. 351-370; *History of civilisations of Central Asia*, vol. V: *Development in contrast: from the sixteenth to the mid-nineteenth century*, ed. Ch. Adle and I. Habib, co-ed. K. Baipakov, UNESCO Publishing, 2003, p. 28-29.

[14] See the geographies of Herodotus (5th c. BC), Strabo and Pliny (1st c. AD), Ptolemy and Arrianus (2nd c. AD).

[15] I.Ju. Krachkovskij, "Arabskaja geographicheskaja literatura [Arabian Geographical Literature]", *in Izbrannye sochinenija* [Selected Works], ed. by V.A. Gordlevskij, Vol. 4, Moscow-Leningrad, 1957, 919 p.; *Bibliotheca Geographorum Arabicorum*, edidit M.J. de Goeje, E.J. Brill, Lugduni Batavorum, E.J. Brill, 1870-1894, 8 vol.

[16] What was known about Central Asia was in some way or other enriched by the accounts of the 13th and 14th century travellers: John Plano Carpino, 1246; John of Carcassonne with André and Guy de Longjumeau, 1249-1251; William of Rubruck, 1253; Thomas of Mancasole, 1329; Nicolò and Maffeo Polo, 1260-1266; Nicolò, Maffeo and Marco Polo, 1271-1291; Odoric of Pordenone, 1318; Pascal of Vittorio with François of Alexandria; Richard of Bourgogne; Gilotto; Laurent of Alexandrie (or of Ancone); Pierre Martele, of Narbonne; Raymond Ruffi (or of Provence), 1338-1339; John of Marignolli or John of Florence; F.B. Pegolotti, 1340; J. Schiltberger, 1394; R.G. de Clavijo, 1403-1406; A. Jenkinson, 1558; B. Goes, 1603-1607; Ph. Avril, 1668; N. Milescu, 1675; and Evert Ysbrants Ides, 1692-1694. For further details see: H. Yule, *Cathay and the way thither, being a collection of medieval notices of China,* new edition, thoroughly revised in the light of recent discoveries by H. Cordier, London, Hakluyt Society, 1914, 3 vol.

[17] R. Kerr, ed., *A general history and collection of voyages and travels, arranged in systematic order: forming a complete history of the origins*

and progress of navigation, discovery, and commerce, by sea and land, from the earliest ages to the present time, Edinburgh, W. Blackwood; [etc.] 1824, 18 v.; V.V. Bartold, "Istorija izuchenija Vostoka v Evrope i v Rossii [A History of Oriental Studies in Europe and Russia]", *Sobranie Sochinenij* [Collected works], t. IX, Moscow, Nauka, 1977 [French version: V.V. Barthold, *La découverte de l'Asie. Histoire de l'orientalisme en Europe et en Russie*, traduction et notes de B. Nikitine, Paris, Payot, 1947]; G. Chaliand, J.-P. Rageau, *Atlas de la découverte du monde* (Cartographie C. Petit), Paris, Fayard, 1984; *Routes d'Asie, marchands et voyageurs XVe-XVIIIe siècle*, actes du Colloque organisé par la Bibliothèque interuniversitaire des langues orientales, Paris, 11-12 décembre 1986, publiés par M. Debout, D. Eeckaute-Bardery et V. Fourniau, Istanbul, Editions ISIS, 1988, 200 p.

[18] With regard to the pre-colonial period (early 18th – the first half of the 19th century) it is important to mention the natural history collections of A. Bekovich-Cherkassky (1716-1718 expedition to Caspian Sea), E.A. Eversman and H.G. Pander (A.F. Negri's 1820 expedition to Bukhara), those of G.S. Karelin: entomological, geological, botanical (a herbarium of the NW Kazakhstan) and ornithological (1832-1836 expedition to the E. and S. Caspian coast); A.I. Schrenck's natural history and ethnographical collections and herbariums (1840 and 1841 expeditions to Djungaria); G.S. Karelin's botanical collection including 1,127 species and 38,000 specimens (1841 expedition to Djungaria and Semirechye); the geological and botanical collections of Colonel G.I. Danilevsky and the naturalist, F.I. Basiner (1843 expedition to Khiva) and the herbariums of Semirechye, collected by A.A. Tatarinov, 1851. In addition to the *Naturalia* there was A. Bekovich-Cherkassky's collection of manuscripts and of archaeological and ethnological objects (T.B. Stanjukovich, "Etnograficheskij muzej Russkogo geograficheskogo obshchestva [Ethnographical Museum of the Russian Geographical Society]", *Trudy Instituta Etnografii im. N.N. Miklukho-Maklaj* [Proceedings of the Institute of Ethnography named after N.N. Miklukho-Maklai, New Series], t. 104, 1977, p. 23), G. Meyendorf's collection of Bukharan coins which also included one medallion (A.F. Negri's 1820 expedition; G. Meyendorf, *Voyage d'Orenbourg à Boukhara, fait en 1820, à travers les steppes qui s'étendent à l'est de la mer d'Aral et au-delà de l'ancien Jaxarte*, Paris, 1826. See the appendices: O.I. Senkovskij, "Opisanie bukharskikh monet" [A Catalogue of Bukharan Coins], p. 309-320; M. Keler, "Opisanie medal'ona, privezennogo iz

Bukhary baronom G. Mejendorfom [A Description of the medal brought from Bukhara by Baron G. Meyendorff], p. 321-328) and a collection of ancient coins made on Colonel G.I. Danilevsky's mission to Khiva, in 1843. For the interpretation of the Meyendorf's collection, see A. Naymark, "The Greeks in Sogdia. Evidence from the Coins", A. Green (ed.), *Land of the Oxus. Studies on Ancient Bactria in Memory of Igor Rubenovich Pichikyan (Miho Museum Publications in South-West and Central Asian Art and Archaeology, 1)*, in print.

[19] B. Vatace, a Greek, 1727; J.G.H. Herber, a German, 1731; K. Miller, a German, 1738-1739; J. Castle (Kestli), an Englishman, 1734-1737; R. Hogg and G. Thompson, Englishmen, 1740-1741; J. Hanway, an Englishman, 1750; Khrisanf, a Greek and Italian, 1793-1795; W. Moorcroft and G. Trebeck, Englishmen, 1819-1825; A. Conolly together with Strong and Willock, Englishmen and a Frenchman, 1829-1830; A. von Humboldt, a German, 1829; A. Burnes, an Englishman, 1831-1833, 1836-1841; J. Wolff, an Englishman, 1831-1934, 1843; H. Wood, an Englishman, 1832; Ch. Stoddart, an Englishman, 1838-1842; J. Abbot, an Englishman, 1839; A.R. Gerngross, a German, 1839; Giovanni, an Italian, 1840; W.T. Thomson, an Englishman, 1840; B. Zaleski, a Pole, 1840; R. Shakespear and A. Conolly, Englishmen, 1840-1842; X. and J.L.A. Hommaire de Hell with J. Laurens, from Alsace, 1848; Th.W. and L. Atkinson, Englishmen, 1848-1852; J.-P. Ferrier, a Frenchman, 1850s. On Occidental travellers in Central Asia, see: S. Gorshenina, *Explorateurs en Asie centrale. Voyageurs et aventuriers de Marco Polo à Ella Maillart*, Genève, Olizane, 2003, 544 p.

[20] Here it is impossible to mention all of the Russian expeditions as they were so numerous, see: O.V. Maslova, *Obzor russkikh puteshestvij i ekspedicij v Srednjuju Aziju (Materialy k bibliografii)* [A Survey of Russian Travels and Expeditions to Central Asia (Bibliographical Materials)], v 4-kh ch., ch.1. 1715-1856 gg. [In 5 Parts. Pt. 1: 1715-1856], Tashkent, 1955, 83 p.; C. Poujol, *La Russie et l'Asie centrale: voyage et expédition de 1714 a 1840*, Thèse de doctorat, Paris, 1985, 462 p.

[21] O. Roy, *L'Asie centrale contemporaine*, Paris, PUF, Que sais-je ?, 2001, p. 21.

[22] M. A. Terent'ev, *Istorija zavoevanija Srednej Azii* [The History of the Conquest of Central Asia], Moscow, 1916, 3 t. See also: S.V. Lurie, *Rossijskaja i Britanskaja imperii na Srednem Vostoke v XIX-nachale XX*

veka: ideologija i praktika [Russian and British Empires in Central Asia in the 19th and early 20th centuries]), PhD thesis, Institut vostokovedenija Rossijskoj Akademii nauk [The Institute for Oriental Studies of the Russian Academy of Sciences], Moscow, 1996; George Joseph Demko, *The Russian colonization of Kazakhstan: 1896-1916*, Ph.D. Geography, The Pennsylvania State University, 1964; G. Kendirbai, *Land and People. The Russian Colonization of the Kazak Steppe*, Berlin, Klaus Schwarz Verlag, 2002.

[23] O.A. Sukhareva, *Bukhara XIX – nachala XX veka* [Bukhara in the 19th and early 20th centuries], Moscow, 1966, p. 99.

[24] P.I. Pashino, "O fabrichnoj i torgovoj dejatel'nosti Turkestanskogo kraja [Industrial and Commercial Activities of the Turkestan Region]", *Izvestija Russkogo Geograficheskogo obshchestva* [Proceedings of Russian Geographical Society], 1867, t. 3, p. 120-139; F. Azadaev, *Tashkent vo vtoroj polovine XIX veka* [Tashkent in the 2nd Half of the 19th Century], Tashkent, 1959, p. 23-24, 32-35, 163.

[25] M.A. Akhunova, *Istorija Kokanda* [A History of Kokand], Tashkent, 1984, p. 6; T.S. Saidkulov, *Samarkand vo vtoroj polovine XIX – nachale XX vekov* [Samarkand in the 2nd Half of the 19th and Early 20th Century], Samarkand, 1970, p. 106.

[26] D.K. Mirzaakhmedov, I.A. Akhrarov, "Privoznaja evropejskaja posuda po materialam bukharskikh kompleksov vtoroj poloviny XVIII - serediny XIX vekov" [Imported European Crockery made with the Materials of Bukharan Complexes of the 2nd Half of the 18th– mid 19th centuries], *Istorija material'noj kul'tury Uzbekistana* [A History of the Material Culture of Uzbekistan], Vol. 20, p. 173-177.

[27] D.K. Mirzaakhmedov, I.A. Akhrarov, *loc. cit.* (note 26), p. 177.

[28] A. Vambery, *Voyages d'un faux derviche dans l'Asie centrale, de Téhéran à Khiva, Bokhara et Samarcand par le grand désert turkoman*, traduit de l'anglais par E.-D. Forgues, Paris, L. Hachette, 1865, p. 160.

[29] E. Schuyler, *Turkestan. Notes taken on a journey to Russian Turkestan, Khokand, Bukhara, and Kuldja*, New York, Scribner, Armstrong & co., 1876, v. I, p. 176.

[30] D. Balland, "Tachkent, métropole de l'Asie centrale ?", *Cahiers d'études sur la Méditerrannée orientale et le monde turco-iranien*, 1997, 24, p. 225-226.

[31] A. Boutroue, *En Transcaspie. Notes de voyages*, Extrait de *l'Annuaire du Club Alpin Français*, Paris, E. Leroux, 1897, p. 35.

[32] For details see: S. Gorshenina, *Explorateurs en Asie centrale, op. cit.* (note 19).

[33] The construction of the Trans-Caspian railway was begun in 1880, under the supervision of General M.N. Annenkov. The first railway lines were those connecting Mikhailov with Kyzyl-Arvat (1881), Ashkhabad (1885), Merv (1886), Bukhara (1887) and Samarkand (1888). In the next part of the project Tashkent was connected with Krasnovodsk (1894), Merv and Kushka (1898), Samarkand and Andijan (1894), Bukhara and Termez (1984). See: Z.K. Akhmedjanova, *K istorii stroitel'stva zheleznykh dorog v Srednej Azii (1880-1917)* [The history of the construction of the railway in Central Asia. 1880-1917], Tashkent, 1965.

[34] S. Gorshenina, "Premiers pas des archéologues russes et français dans le Turkestan russe (1870-1890): méthodes de recherche et destin des collections", *Cahiers du Monde Russe*, Paris, 1999, N° 3 (40) juillet-septembre, p. 365-384.

[35] See, for example: V.V. Bartold', "K voprosy ob arkheologicheskikh nakhodkakh [About archaeological finds]", *Sobranie sochinenij* [Collected Works], t. 4, Moscow, 1966, p. 126-127: in 1904, the trade in antiques "is perfectly organized; brokers form a serried syndicate, and all the threads are joined in the hands of one man; on the surface, however, the brokers are working independently from each other. A certain Mr B comes to your suite in the hotel, offers you 'antiques' and persuades you to purchase them only from him and not from certain Mr A, whose improper methods (which you have already seen) he, Mr B, cannot approve; meanwhile, there is a full agreement between Messrs A and B, and Mr B delivers received money to the same Mr A" (translation of A. Naymark, *loc. cit.* [note 18]). For a photograph see Cherevanskij, *Dve volny* [The Two Waves], Saint-Petersburg, 1898.

[36] G.N. Chabrov, *Istorija muzejnogo dela v Srednej Azii (dorevolju-cionnyj period)* [The History of Museums in Central Asia (before the revolution)], manuscript from 1950-1951, CGA RUz, F. R-2681, cat. 1, file 42, p. 20. See also: CGA RUz, F. I-1, cat. 19, file 892, p. 14, 15.

[37] E. Markov, "Fergana. Putevye ocherki Kokandskogo khanstva" [Ferghana. Travel Sketches of the Kokand Khanate], *Russkij vestnik* [Russian Herald], 1893, t. 9; V.L. Vjatkin, "Ob arkheologicheskikh

nakhodkakh v Samarkande [On archaeological finds in Samarkand]",
Samarkand, 8/21.VI.1904, N° 29.

[38] V.V. Krestovskij, *V gostjakh u emira Bukharskogo* [A Visit to the
Emir of Bukhara], Saint-Petersburg, 1887, cited from G.N. Chabrov, *op.
cit.* (note 36), p. 35.

[39] A. Vambery, *op. cit.* (note 28), p. 167.

[40] For one of the earliest detailed descriptions of the market in Bukhara
see: L.F. Kostenko, *Puteshestvie v Bukharu russkoj missii v 1870 godu s
marshrutom ot Tashkenta do Bukhary L.F. Kostenko* [A trip undertaken by
the Russian mission from Tashkent to Bukhara in 1870], Saint-Petersburg,
1871: *Turkestanskij sbornik* [A Turkestanian collection of papers and stud-
ies], *op.cit.* (note 6), t. 32], p. 65-67. Of some interest is the description by
E. Schuyler, *op. cit.* (note 29), v. I, p. 173-224.

[41] A. Boutroue, *loc. cit.* (note 31), p. 23.

[42] V.L. Vjatkin, "Bukharskij knizhnyj rynok [Book Market in
Bukhara]", *Turkestanskie Vedomosti* [The Turkestanian News], 1897, N°
61.

[43] P. Uvarova, "Poezdka v Tashkent i Samarkand [A trip to Tashkent
and Samarkand]", *Russkaja mysl'* [Russian Thought], Vol. 10, Moscow,
1891, p. 1-19; t. 12, 1891, p. 1-25; *Eadem*, "Oblastnye muzei [Regional
Museums]", *Trudy XII arkheologicheskogo s'ezda v Jaroslavle*
[Proceedings of the 12th Archaeological Congress in Yaroslavl], t. 2,
Moscow, 1891, p. 323-324.

[44] A.A. Semenov, "Nechto o sredneaziatskikh gemmakh, ikh ljubitel-
jakh i sobiratel jakh (Iz vospominanij proshlogo) [Some notes on Central
Asian gems, amateurs and collections, memoirs]", *Izvestija otdelenija
obshchestvennykh nauk AN TadzhSSR* [Proceedings of the Department of
Social Sciences of the Academy of Sciences of the Tajik SSR], Vol. 14,
1957, p. 145; M.E. Masson, "Kratkij ocherk istorii izuchenija Srednej Azii
v arkheologicheskom otnoshenii [A Short Survey of the History of
Archaeological Research in Central Asia]", *Trudy Sredneaziatskogo
Gosudarstvennogo Universiteta. Arkheologija Srednej Azii* [Proceedings
of the Central Asian State University. Central Asian Archaeology],
Tashkent, 1956, p. 145.

[45] Shubinskij, *Ocherki Bukhary* [Bukharan Sketches], Saint-
Petersburg, 1892.

⁴⁶ A. Boutroue, *loc. cit.* (note 31), p. 23.

⁴⁷ H. Moser, *A travers l'Asie centrale. La Steppe Kirghise - Le Turkestan russe - Boukhara - Khiva - Le Pays des Turcomans et la Perse. Impressions de voyage*, Paris, E. Plon, Nourrit et C°, 1885, p. 172.

⁴⁸ A. Boutroue, *loc. cit.* (note 31), p. 29.

⁴⁹ P. Bernard, "Maracanda-Afrasiab colonie grecque", *in La Persia e l'Asia Centrale da Alessandro al X secolo*, actes du colloque, Accademia Nationale dei Lincei, Roma, 1996, p. 331-365

⁵⁰ *Expédition française en Russie, en Sibérie et dans le Turkestan par Ch. E. de Ujfalvy de Mezö Kövesd*, vol. [1] *Le Kohistan, le Ferghanah et Kouldja*, avec un appendice sur la Kachqharie, Paris, E. Leroux, 1878, p. 52.

⁵¹ A.A. Semenov, "Nechto...", *loc. cit.* (note 44), p. 145; *Idem, Khudozhestvennaja rukopis' na territorii sovremennogo Uzbekistana* [Illuminated Manuscripts on the Territory of Central Asia Today], a manuscript from 1948. The archives of the Institute of Fine Art, Khamza in Tashkent.

⁵² E.A. Beze, *Putevoditel' po Central'noj Azii* [A Guide to Central Asia], Moscow, 1888.

⁵³ V.G. Moshkova, *Kovry narodov Srednej Azii* [Carpets of the Peoples of Central Asia], Tashkent, Fan, 1970.

⁵⁴ Cited from M. Durdyev, "Vozvratjatsja li v Turkmenistan nacional'nye cennosti ? [Will National Values be Returned to Turmenistan?]", *Kontakt,* Ashkhabad, 6.03.1992.

⁵⁵ A.A. Semenov, "Po granicam Bukhary i Afganistana (Putevye ocherki 1898 goda) [Along the Borders to Bukhara and Afghanistan. Travel Notes from 1898]", *Istoricheskij vestnik* [Historical Review], t. 87-88, 1902.

⁵⁶ For information on archaeological discoveries in the region, which scientists call Northern Bactria, see B.A. Litvinskij, *La civilisation de l'Asie centrale antique*, Rahden /Westf.: Leidorf, 1998 (Archäologie in Iran und Turan; Bd. 3), 215 p., B. Ja. Stavisky, *La Bactriane sous les Kushans. Problèmes d'histoire et de culture*, transl. by P. Bernard, M. Burda, F. Grenet, P. Leriche, Paris, 1986, 322 p. (in Russian: Moscow, 1977); *idem, Sud'by buddizma v Sredneij Azii [The fate of Buddhism in Central Asia]*, Moscow, Vostochnaja literatura, 1998, 214 p.

⁵⁷ *Srednjaja Azija*. Al'manakh. Nauchno-literaturnyj sbornik s kalendarem na 1896 god, pod. red. E.T. Smirnova [*Central Asia*. An Almanac. Miscellany of Research and Literary Works with a Calender from the year 1896, ed. by E.T. Smirnov], Tashkent, 1895.

⁵⁸ A.A. Semenov, "Nechto...", *loc. cit.* (note 44), p. 145.

⁵⁹ M. Monnier, *Itinéraire à travers l'Asie, levé au cours du voyage accompli durant les années 1895, 1896, 1897, 1898 sur l'initiative et pour le compte du journal LE TEMPS; publiés sous le patronage de la Société de Géographie avec le concours du ministère de l'Instruction publique et des Beaux-Arts*, Paris, Plon-Nourrit et C°, 1900, p. 161.

⁶⁰ H. Moser, *op. cit.* (note 47), p. 105, 259.

⁶¹ N.I. Veselovskij, "Sushchestvujut li v Srednej Azii poddelki drevnostej ? [Are There Counterfeit Antiques in Central Asia?]", *Zapiski Vostochnogo Otdelenija Russkogo arkheologicheskogo Obshchestva* [Transactions conducted by the Oriental Department of Russian Archaeological Society], t. 1, Saint-Petersburg, 1887, p. 110-114.

⁶² M.E. Masson's observation. See: CGA RUz, F. R-2681, cat. 1, f. 1065, p. 1.

⁶³ See e.g.: I.P. Jampol'skij, *Kustarnoe delo. 1. Kustarnye promysly Turkestana – Aziatskaja Rossija* [Handicrafts. 1. Handicrafts of Turkestan – Russian Asia], t. 2, Saint-Petersburg, 1914. About figurines see V.V. Bartold, *loc. cit.* (note 35), p. 127; E.K. Kverfel'd, *Keramika Blizhnego Vostoka* [Ceramics of the Near East], Leningrad, 1947.

⁶⁴ V.A. Shishkin, "K istorii arkheologicheskogo izuchenija Samarkanda i ego okrestnostej [About the archaeological study of Samarkand and its surroundings]", *Afrasiab I*, Tashkent, 1969, p. 38; V.L. Vjatkin, *loc. cit.* (note 37); A. Naymark, *loc. cit.* (note 18), n. 51.

⁶⁵ *Turkestanskie Vedomosti* [The Turkestanian News], 1906, N° 101; A.A. Semenov, "Pis'mennosti sushchestvovavshie v Srednej Azii [Types of Writing Which Existed in Central Asia]", *Izvestija Tadzhikskogo filiala AN SSSR* [Transactions conducted by the Tajik Department of the Academy of Sciences of the USSR], 1946, N° 12.

⁶⁶ P. Bernard, "A propos de quelques faux dans l'histoire des cultes de l'Asie centrale", *Cultes et monument religieux dans l'Asie centrale préislamique*, sous la dir. de F. Grenet, Editions du CNRS, 1987, p. 23-28.

⁶⁷ P. Bernard, *loc. cit.* (note 66), p. 27.

68 M.E. Masson, "Po povodu dalekogo proshlogo Samarkanda [On the Remote Past of Samarkand]", *Iz istorii iskusstva velikogo goroda* [From the History of Art of the Great City], Tashkent, 1972, p. 29-30. About one Egyptian object of the Kastalsky's collection see also B.B. Piotrovskij, "Drevne-Egipetskie predmety, najdenye na territorii Sovetskogo Sojuza" [Ancient Egyptian objects found on the territory of USSR], *Sovetskaja Arkheologija*, 1958, N° 1, p. 22. * See also *Addenda, infra*, p. 205.

68b P. Bernard, "Un nouveau livre sur les Parthes", *Studia Iranica*, 8, 1979, p. 135-139.

69 O. Lobri, "Iz Turkestanskikh vospominanij" [From Memoirs about Turkestan], *Russkij vestnik* [The Russian Herald], 1895; V. Dukhovskaya, *Turkestanskie vospominanija* [Turkestan Memoirs], Saint-Petersburg, 1913; see also V.I. Masalskij, *Turkestanskij Kraj*, St-Pb., 1913, p. 529.

70 "Muzei v Turkmenii [Museums in Turkmenia]", *Etnograficheskoe obozrenie* [The Ethnographical Review], 1907, N° 1-2.

71 V.A. Prishchepova, *Kollekcii zagovorili. Istorija formirovanija kollekcij Muzeja antropologii i etnografii [Kunstkamera] po Srednej Azii i Kazaxstanu (1870-1940)* [Collections begin to speak. History of the formation of the collection about Central Asia and Kazakhstan (1870-1940) in the Mueum of Anthropology and Ethnography], Saint-Petersburg, 2000, p. 53.

72 A.A. Fal'kerzam, "Starinnye kovry Srednej Azii [Old Carpets of Central Asia]", *Starye gody* [The Old Years], 1914, October-December.

73 O. Lobri, *loc. cit.* (note 69).

74 E. Markov, *Rossija v Srednej Azii. Ocherki puteshestvija po Zakavkaz'ju, Turkmenii, Bukhare, Samarkandskoj, Tashkentskoj i Ferganskoj oblastjam, Kaspijskomu morju i Volge* [Russia in Central Asia. Notes on Travels in the Transcaucasian Region, Turkmenia, Bukhara, Samarkand, Tashkent and Fergana Regions], Saint-Petersburg, 1901.

75 G.N. Chabrov, *Istorija..., op. cit.* (note 36), p. 42.

76 M.E. Masson's observations (note 62).

77 H. Moser, *op.cit* (note 47), p. 105.

78 A.A. Semenov, "Nechto...", *loc. cit.* (note 44), p. 145.

79 1888, 5 March, N° 65. Also V.V. Bartold, *loc. cit.* (note 35), p. 126.

80 A.A. Semenov, "Pis'mennosti...", *loc. cit.* (note 65).

[81] *Otchet Imperatorskoj publichnoj biblioteki za 1871 god* [A Report by the Imperial Public Library for the Year 1871], Saint-Petersburg, 1872, p. 14-22.

[82] *Voprosy predlagaemye Imperatorskim Russkim Geograficheskim obshchestvom pri issledovanii Khivinskogo khanstva i sopredel'nykh s nim stran v geograficheskom, etnograficheskom i kul'turno-istoricheskom otnoshenii*, sost. P.I. Lerkhom [The Questions Proposed by the Imperial Russian Geographical Society for the Study of the Khiva Khanate and the Adjacent Lands in Geographical, Ethnographic, Historical and Cultural Respects, by P.I. Lerch], Saint-Petersburg, 1873, p. 1-37.

[83] P.P. Ivanov, *Arkhiv khivinskikh khanov [The Archives of the Khans of Khiva]*, Leningrad, 1940.

[84] A. Erkinov et Sh. Vahidov, "Une source méconnue pour l'étude de la production de livres à la cour de Muhammad Rahîm Khân II (Khiva, fin XIXe s.), *Cahiers de l'Asie centrale*, n° 7, 1999, p. 177. See also: B.V. Lunin, *Srednjaja Azija v dorevoljucionnom i sovetskom vostokovedenii* [Central Asia in Pre-Revolutionary and Soviet Oriental Studies], Tashkent, 1965, p. 119-120.

[85] *Turkestanskie Vedomosti* [The Turkestanian News], 1873, N° 50; A.L. Kun, "Opisanie pechatej khivinskikh khanov" [A Description of the Seals of the Khans of Khiva], *Ibidem*, 1873, N° 40; *Idem*, "Nauchnye raboty vo vremja Khivinskogo pokhoda" [Research Work during the Khiva Expedition], *Ibidem*, 1873, N° 50.

[86] According to M.E. Masson, these stamps, which had hitherto been considered as lost, were later found in the Saint-Petersburg Public Library (note 62).

[87] V. Stasov, "Tron khivinskikh khanov [The Throne of the Khans of Khiva]", *Vestnik izjashchnykh iskusstv* [The Journal of Fine Arts], Vol. 4, Part. 5, Saint-Petersburg, 1886, p. 405-410.

[88] V.S. Ikonnikov, *Opyt russkoj istoriografii* [An Essay on Russian Historiography], t. 1, Kiev, 1891. * See also *Addenda, infra*, p. 205.

[89] A.I. Svirskij, *Istorija moej zhizni* [My Life-Story], Sverdlovsk, 1964, p. 417; *Katalog kartin [...] knjaza Nikolaja Konstantinovicha, op. cit.* (note 7); *Opisanie Khivinskogo pokhoda 1873 goda po materialam osoboj komissii, utverzhdennoj totchas posle pokhoda pod predsedatel'stvom byvshego nachal'nika polevogo shtaba*, sostovleno

polkovnikom F.I. Lobysevichem pod redakciej general-ad'jutanta V.N. Trockogo [An Account of the Khiva Expedition of 1873 based on Materials from the Special Committee, Appointed Immediately after the Expedition and Presided over by the Former Head of the Field Headquarters. Written by Colonel F.I. Lobysevich under the supervision of Adjutant-General V.N. Trotsky], Saint-Petersburg, 1898, 293 p.

[90] On the manuscript of I.N. Glushkov about Turkmen jewellery: V.A. Prishchepova, *op.cit.* (note 71), p. 45.

[91] Exhibited at Turkestan Exhibition of 1909: *Katalog voennogo otde-lenija Turkestanskoj promyshlennoj, sel'sko-khozjajstvennoj, nauchnoj i khudozhestvennoj vystavki, 1909 god* [A Catalogue of the Military Department of the Turkestan Industrial, Agricultural, Scientific and Art Exhibition of 1909], Tashkent, 1909.

[92] A.L. Troickaja, "Arkhiv kokandskikh khanov XIX veka. Predvaritel'nyj obzor [The Archives of the Kokand Khans of the 19th Century. Preliminary Survey]", *Trudy Gosudarstvennoj publichnoj biblioteki im. M.E. Saltykova-Shchedrina* [Proceedings of the State Public Library named after M.E. Saltykov-Shchedrin], t. 2 (5), Leningrad, 1957, p. 189; *Eadem, Katalog arkhivov kokandskikh khanov XIX veka* [A Catalogue of the Archives of the Kokand Khans of the 19th century], Moscow, 1968.

[93] *Turkestanskie Vedomosti* [The Turkestanian News], 1888, N° 46.

[94] See note 324.

[95] A.T., "Chernjaevskij muzej (Po sluchaju 50-letnogo jubileja zavoevanija Tashkenta)" [Chernyaev Museum. On the Occasion of the 50th Anniversary of the Conquest of Tashkent], *Voenno-Istoricheskij sbornik* [Military and Historical Almanac], 5th Year, 1915, N° 3. A Free Supplement to the 9th issue of *Voennyj sbornik* [Military Almanac], p. 97.

[96] A. Muminov, "Fonds nationaux et collections privées de manuscrits en écriture arabe de l'Ouzbékistan", *Cahiers d'Asie centrale,* n° 7, 1999, p. 18.

[97] H. Moser, *op.cit.* (note 47), p. 86-87; V. Dukhovskaya, *op. cit.* (note 69); A.A. Semenov, "Kovry russkogo Turkestana [The Carpets of Russian Turkestan]", *Etnograficheskoe obozrenie* [Ethnographical Review], Moscow, t. 88-89, 1911, N° 1-2, p. 137-167 (a reprint: Moscow, 1911, 43 p.) with an appendix "Supplementary Bibliography" and "An Index of the

Bibliography on Central Asian Carpets".

[98] *Op.cit.* (note 62).

[99] Collection Nr. 2619 and 3687: V.A. Prishchepova, *op. cit.* (note 71), p. 105-106. Collection Nr. 313, 2971, 2973, 2687: S.P. Rusejkina, "Muzejnye etnograficheskie fondy kak istochnik dlja sostavlenija istoriko-etnograficheskogo atlasa Srednej Azii i Kazakhstana. Materialy k istoriko-etnograficheskomu atlasu Srednej Azii i Kazakhstana [Museum of Ethnographical Finds as a Source for a Historico-Ethnographical Atlas of Central Asia and Kazakhstan]", *Trudy instituta etnografii im. N.N. Miklukho-Maklaja, Novaja serija* [Proceedings of the Institute of Ethnography named after N.N. Miklukho-Maklai, New Series], t. XVIII, Moscow-Leningrad, 1961, p. 47.

[100] S.P. Rusejkina, *loc.cit.* (note 99), p. 47, 49, 79; V.A. Prishchepova, *op.cit.* (note 71), p. 13-14.

[101] Collection of the Museum of Ethnography in Saint-Petersburg, Nr. 4186, 4457, 4463, 4467, 4469, 4646, 4651, 4705, 5148, 5155, 5183, 5474, 5899 (489 objects): S.P. Rusejkina, *loc.cit.* (note 99), p. 49.

[102] H. Moser, *op.cit.* (note 47), p. 87-88, 153, 159, 161-162, 165-166, 177, 182, 202-203, 249-250, 259.

[103] CGA RUz, F. I-3 [Fund of the Russian political agent in Bukhara], c. 1, f. 43, p. 168-173, 193). S. Gorshenina, "On khotel sokhranit' incognito (Puteshestvie ital'janskogo princa Victora Emmanuelja v Srednjuju Aziju) [He wanted to preserve his disguise (Journey of Italian prince, Victor-Emmanuel, to Central Asia)]", *Zvezda Vostoka* [The Star of the Orient], 2002, N° 2, p. 177-179.

[104] H. Moser, *op.cit.* (note 47), p. 165-166, 263.

[105] S.P. Rusejkina, *loc. cit.* (note 99), p. 39; V.A. Prishchepova, *op.cit.* (note 71), p. 33-34.

[106] V.A. Prishchepova, *op.cit.* (note 71), p. 105-106.

[107] The West European collectors of natural objects were: F. Xaver von Schwarz, a German (entomological collection, 1874 – early1880s); A. Edmund Brehm and O. Finsch, Germans (herbariums, zoological collections, 1876); J. Martin, a Frenchman (collection of plants and animals, specimens of minerals, 1879-1886, 1889-1892); C. Saaro, a German (collections of insects, 1891-1897); E. de Poncins, a Frenchman (collection of stuffed highland animals and birds, 1893-1894; "K. Rosst", an

Englishman, 1898; "K.R. Goldovitch Stahl von Holstein", a Finn, 1912-1913; "K. von Menzenkampf", a Finn, 1912-1913; "E.M. Wolf", a Finn, 1912-1913.

Among the Russian collectors of natural objects were: Kh. Pander, A. Eversman, 1820; G.S. Karelin (one of the largest herbariums of Kazakhstan, entomological, geological, botanical and ornithological collections from Djungaria and Semirechye; its duplicates were partly distributed in Russia and abroad); A.I. Schrenck (botanical collections of 1840); A.A. Tatarinov (a herbarium of Semirechye, 1851); N.A. Severtsev (botanical, zoological and geological collections of the Pamirs, 1857, 1865-1866, 1874, 1877); O.A. and A.P. Fedchenko (botanical and zoological collections, 1868-1869); P. Doroshin (a collection of fossils, 1869); Colonel Stoletov (herbarium of Khiva, 1869-1870); G.I. Radle (a collection of bugs and molluscs, plants and animals, 1870); V.I. Markozov (botanical collections, 1871); N.I. Grodekov (a botanical collection, 1873); S.M. Mikhajlovich, M.N. Bogdanov, N.P. Barbot-de-Marny, 1874; M.D. Skobelev (a collection of plants and animals, 1876); V.F. Russov (zoological collections, 1877); Samara research expedition of 1879; V.F. Oshanin (botanical, zoological and entomological collections, 1885); A.E. Regel (botanical and mineralogical collections, 1881-1883); G.E. Grum-Grzhymailo (zoological and entomological collections, 1885); N.A. Zarudny (zoological collections, 1884); N.B. Sorokin (botanical collections, 1884); A.M. Nikol'skij, 1855; A.N. Krasnov (geological and botanical collections, 1886) and others.

[108] V.L. Vjatkin, "Bukharskij knizhnyj rynok", *loc. cit.* (note 42). According to A.A. Semenov, agents of the Iranian Prince, Madjid Saltan, bought manuscripts and miniatures in Turkestan for him (note 44). Lerch pointed out that in 1909 Bukharan merchants directly supplied coins to the Moscow collector Lisenkov (quoted from A. Naymark, *loc. cit.* [note 18], n. 40).

[109] M. Durdyev, *loc. cit.* (note 54).

[110] G.N. Chabrov, *Istorija...*, *op. cit.* (note 36), p. 32.

[111] D. Evarnickij, "K voprosu ob utverzhdenii v Samarkande muzeja drevnostej [On Establishing a Museum of Antiques in Samarkand]", *Okraina* [Periphery], 28.06.1893, N° 86.

[112] V.V. Bartold, *loc. cit.* (note 35), p. 129.

[113] N.S. Sadykova, *Muzejnoe delo v Uzbekistane* [Museums in

Uzbekistan: Their Organization and Functioning], Tashkent, 1975.

[114] Ch.-E. Ujfalvy, a Frenchman: an analysis of the ruins of the fortress of Djankent [Yangikent, near Kazalinsk]; excavations and a visit to the Mausoleum of Khodja Ahmad Yassavi in the city of Turkestan; a survey of the site of Ak-Tepe, near Marghilan; collecting of surface archaeological material at the site of the Pendjikent; excavations at Afrasiab / Samarkand, 1876-1877, 1879, 1881. G. Bonvalot, a Frenchman: a number of excavations in Termez on his third expedition in 1886. L. de Beylié, a Frenchman: archaeological surveys, 1888. O. Olufsen, a Dane: surveys in the Pamir Region, 1889. E. Blanc, a Frenchman: numerous surveys and excavations in Samarkand, 1890-1892, 1894-1895. O. Donner, K. Munsk, Finns: monuments of the ancient Turks near Aulia-Ata and Verny, 1890-1900. A. Heikel, a Finn: excavations of nomadic kurgans in the Talas Valley, surveys to the North of Tashkent, 1898-1899); "K.R.G. Stal' fon Golshteïn", "K.K. fon Menzenkampf", "E.M. Volf", Finns: surveys, 1912-1913. J. Chaffanjon: excavations at Merv, Paykend, Samarkand (Afrasiab), exploration of the ruins of Akyr-Tach, 1894-1895. R. Pumpelly: excavations of Anau in Turkmenistan, 1903-1904. J.A. Castagné: numerous surveys and excavations in the Orenburg Province and in Turkestan, 1912-1921.

[115] Frenchman E. Masson (voyage of 1892), having at his disposal a specially equipped carriage for his trip to Merv, made a collection thanks to the help of the former Russian Ambassador to Paris, General M.N. Annenkov, and that of Captain Andreyev. J. Chaffanjon (1894-1895) not only had permission to make excavations, but also had a special carriage equipped on the orders of General Kuropatkin, with the right to run all the way through the Trans-Caspian Region. Chaffanjon himself told of the Russian generals and consuls being very helpful to the French research mission: General Kashtalinsky, a passionate collector of antiques, showed the ruins of old Merv to the French; Captain Korolkov, Head of Artillery in Prjevalsk, informed them about the results of 30-year-long observations of the tidal dynamics of the Issyk-Kul; the Governor-General of the city of Verny Ivanov put official statistics on colonization rates and a series of meteorological observations at their disposal; N.A. Pantusov and P.V. Gurde accompanied J. Chaffanjon during his exploration of the Nestorian cemetery near Verny; Russian consuls and businessmen were the first people he met on his voyage to Mongolia and China. See: French National Archives, Fond F 17 / 2946 / 2; J. Chaffanjon, "Rapport sur une mission scientifique dans l'Asie centrale et la Sibérie", *Nouvelles archives des mis-*

sions scientifiques et littéraires, Choix de rapports et instructions, publié sous les auspices du Ministère de l'Instruction publique et des Beaux-Arts, t. IX, Paris, Impr. nationale, MDCCC XCIX (1899), p. 55-56, 61, 63, 64, 67, 72, 77, 82.

[116]Russian military geographical and topographical maps were, e.g. at the disposal of the French travellers E. Blanc in 1890-1892 and 1894-1895, J. Chaffanjon in 1894-1895, the Italians Sc. Borghese and J. Brocherel in 1900, and the American expedition, led by R. Pumpelly in 1903-1904.

[117]The Dane O. Olufsen, and the Frenchmen E. Blanc, J. Chaffanjon, and Ch.-E. Ujfalvy (CGA RUz, F. I-1, c. 20, f. 8791, p. 3, 18, 20) were given the right to take large collections abroad. Between November 1895 and June 1897, Chaffanjon sent fifty-three cases, containing various collections (3,584 objects) to France. The French National Archives, Fond F 17 / 17270, p. 1-4; *Bulletin de la Société entomologique de France*, rapport du 8 décembre 1897, p. 297-300. On the other hand, according to V.V. Bartold, the Russian political agent in Bukhara A.D. Kolmakov published at the station of the city a placard mentioning the interdiction of antics exportation from the Khanate: V.V. Bartold, *loc. cit.* (note 35), p. 129, n. 4.

[118]E.g., E. Blanc, who represented France at the International exhibition in Nizhnij Novgorod in 1896, received - as a gift for the Muséum d'histoire naturelle and the Trocadéro - 47 cases of various collections from the Russian Government and high-ranking officials of the Siberian Province (Tobolsk, Irkutsk, Omsk and Blagoveshchensk).

[119]Ch.-E. Ujfalvy, *Expédition...*, *op. cit.* (note 50), vol. I, p. IV-V.

[120]Quoted from B.V. Lunin, "Samarkandskij ljubitel' stariny i sobiratel' drevnostej Mîrzâ Bukhari [Samarkand Devotee and Collector of Antiques - Mîrzâ Bukhari]", *Obshchestvennye nauki v Uzbekistane* [Social Sciences in Turkestan], 1963, N° 6, p. 35.

[121]V.A. Prishchepova, *op.cit.* (note 71), p. 34.

[122]M. de Ujfalvy-Bourdon, *De Paris à Samarcande, le Ferghanah, le Kouldja et la Sibérie occidentale, impressions de voyage d'une parisienne*, Paris, Hachette, 1880, p. 121-122, 130, 180, 210, 316.

[123]See, e.g.: M. Durdyev, *loc. cit.* (note 54).

[124]Rusejkina, *loc.cit.* (note 99), p. 40.

[125]Rusejkina, *loc.cit.* (note 99), p. 42.

[126]N. Makarenko, *Khudozhestvennye sokrovishcha Imperatorskogo*

Ermitazha, Kratkij putevoditel' [Artistic Treasures of the Imperial Hermitage. A short Guidebook], Saint-Petersburg, 1916; B.V. Lunin, "Samarkandskij ljubitel' [...] Mîrzâ Bukhari", *loc. cit.* (note 120), p. 36, 39; A.Ju. Jakubovskij, "Sredneaziatskie sobranija Ermitazha i ikh znachenie dlja izuchenija istorii kul'tury i iskusstva Srednej Azii do XVI veka [Central Asian Collections of the Hermitage and Their Importance for the Study of the Culture and Arts of Central Asia before the 16ᵗʰ Century]", *Trudy Otdela istorii kul'tury i iskusstva Vostoka Gosudarstvennogo Ermitazha* [Proceedings of the Department of Oriental Culture and Art of the Hermitage], t. II, Leningrad, 1940, p. 8; A. Banck, *infra*, p. 205.

[127]E. Gafferberg, N. Kisljakov, "Otdel Perednej i Srednej Azii Instituta etnografii AN SSSR (The Department of Near and Central Asia of the Institute of Ethnography, the Academy of Sciences of the USSR)", *Sovetskaja etnografija* [Soviet Ethnography], 1948, N° 1; V.A. Prishchepova, *op.cit.* (note 71).

[128]Collections Nr. 2871, 2971, 2973: V.A. Prishchepova, *op.cit.* (note 71), p. 95-96.

[129]V.A. Prishchepova, *op.cit.* (note 71), p. 86-95.

[130]V.A. Prishchepova, *op.cit.* (note 71), p. 96-99.

[131]S.P. Rusejkina, *loc. cit.* (note 99), p. 41.

[132]S.P. Rusejkina, *loc.cit.* (note 99), p. 76.

[133]Collections of the Museum of Oriental Cultures in Moscow, Nr. 14 and 600-635: S.P. Rusejkina, *loc.cit.* (note 99), p. 67.

[134]Rusejkina, *loc.cit.* (note 99), p. 42-46; V.A. Prishchepova, *op.cit.* (note 71), p. 95-96.

[135]*T'oung pao*, Leiden, E.J. Brill, vol. II, 1891, p. 439-441.

[136]*Revue de France*, t. 24, Paris, 1877, p. 223.

[137]S. Gorshenina, "Turkestanskie puteshestvija Sharlja-Euzhena Uzhfalvy [Travels in Turkestan of Charles-Eugène Ujfalvy]", *Kul'turnye cennosti-1997-1998* [Cultural Values], *Bibliotheca Turkmennica*, Saint-Petersburg, European House, 1999, p. 227-234.

[138]F. Richard, "Manuscrits persans de la Bibliothèque nationale de France se rapportant à l'Asie centrale musulmane", *Cahiers d'Asie centrale*, n° 7, 1999, p. 57-63.

[139]They are registered as *manuscrits* in the *Supplément persan* under

N° 1671-1737: F. Richard, *loc.cit* (note 138).

[140]They are listed in the *Supplément persan* under N° 2005-2039: F. Richard, *loc.cit.* (note 138).

[141]*Supplément persan* N° 2062-2072): F. Richard, *loc.cit.* (note 138).

[142]F. Richard, *loc.cit.* (note 138).

[143]From information provided by B.A. Litvinsky.

[144]From information provided by B.A. Litvinsky.

[145]O.M. Dalton, *The Treasure of the Oxus with Other Examples of early Oriental Metal-Work*, London, 1964 [3]; E.V. Zejmal', *Amudar 'inskij klad*. Katalog vystavki [The Treasure of the Amu-Darya. An Exhibition Catalogue], Leningrad, 1979.

[146]An extreme example of such an exception was Gulbenkian, whose collections, hidden from everyone's eyes in his residence in Avenue Iéna in Paris, were inaccessible to everybody during his lifetime.

[147]*Turkestanskie Vedomosti* [The Turkestanian News], 1909, N° 144; G.N. Chabrov, *Istorija...*, *op. cit.* (note 36), p. 59; A.I. Svirskij, *op. cit.* (note 89), p. 456-464.

[148]R.N. Balsiger, E.J. Kläy, *Bei Schah, Emir und Khan. Henri Moser Charlottenfels. 1844-1923*, Schaffhausen, Meier Verlag, 1992.

[149]Among the western travellers who presented their collections at the meeting of learned societies or congresses, we must mention: E. Blanc (International Anthropological Congress in Moscow [1892], Société de géographie de Paris, Congrès national de géographie à Tours [1893]); G. Bonvalot (Société de géographie de Paris); J. Chaffanjon (Société de géographie de Paris); E.-C. Croizier (Comité des travaux historiques et scientifiques, Société de géographie de Marseille); H. Krafft (Société de géographie de Paris, Académie française, Académie nationale de Reims); E. Masson (Chambre de commerce de Lyon); R. Pumpelly (Carnegie Institution of Washington); Ch.-E. Ujfalvy (the Imperial Society of Friends of Natural Sciences, Anthropology and Ethnography, Moscow, Société de géographie de Paris), etc.

[150]In 1883 V.V. Vereshchagin exhibited in the German Club in Moscow, together with his own works, some objects from his collections made in Turkestan, India and Turkey (*Perepiska P.M. Tret'jakova i V.V. Stasova. 1874-1897* [Correspondence between P.M. Tretyakov and V.V. Stasov. 1874-1897], Moscow-Leningrad, 1949).

[151] See Appendix I.

[152] In Kaufmann's collections at the Moscow Museum of the Peoples of the USSR: S.P. Rusejkina, *loc. cit.* (note 99), p. 50.

[153] *Petit journal*, 1897, 30 juillet. For information about this exhibition see also *L'Evénement*, 1897, 30 juillet.

[154] E.I. Aleksander, G.A. Arendorenko, V.L. Vyatkin, N.I. Veselovsky, N.I. Grodekov, S.M. Dudin, S.M. Dukhovskoy, E.F. Kal', I.N. Glushkov, Ja.S Edelstein, J. Castagné, B.N. Kastalsky, K.P. von Kaufmann, I.I. Krause, P.I. Lerch, K.N. de Lazari, N.S. Lykoshin, S.M. Nizhansky, S.F. Nikolai, Mishchenko, K.E. and P.E. Ostrovskikh, N.P. Ostroumov, V.F. Oshanin, N.F. Petrovsky, K.N. Pos'et, A.N. Samoilovich, O.A. Fedchenko, Ju.D. Juzhakov, I.N. Rachinsky, G.A. Nasibianc, V.D. Pelc and others.

[155] The following were distinguished for their generous donations: H. Moser, who gave his collection of arms, harness, clothes, fabric, jewellery, ceramics and manuscripts (4,000 items altogether) and some albums of photographs to the Museum of History, in Bern; H. Krafft, who donated some of his oriental collections to the Museum of Decorative Arts in Paris and to the Louvre; L. Mangini, who donated to the Museum of Natural History in Paris, L.S. Barszscewski's collection, bought in Turkestan by J. Chaffanjon; H.-R. d'Allemagne, who donated a fragment of grave stelae from Samarkand (14th-15th c.) to the Section islamique of the Louvre; E. Hindamian, who brought from Samarkand, 13 Nestorian stelae from the 13th-14th centuries, found in Semirechye by F.V. Poyarkov and Andreyev in 1886 and donated by them, together with other objects (inscribed tablets and vases) to the Musée Guimet in Paris in 1912.

[156] Cited from B.V. Lunin, "Samarkandskij ljubitel' [...] Mirza Bukhari", *loc. cit.* (note 120), p. 35.

[157] Cited from B.V. Lunin, "Samarkandskij jubitel' [...] Mirza Bukhari", *loc. cit.* (note 120), p. 37, 38-39.

[158] He set up, in his private residence in Reims, a museum called the Musée-Hôtel Le Vergeur, which was - according to his testament – donated to the city with all its collections (various ethnographical collections, photographs and publications). The museum is administered by "La Société des amis du vieux Reims", founded in 1909.

[159] CGA RUz, F. I-72, cat. 1, f. 26; *Turkestanskie Vedomosti* [The Turkestanian News], 1891, September 24; Protokoly Turkestanskogo

kruzhka ljubitelej arkheologii ot 1/II-1897 [Proceedings of the Turkestanian Circle of Friends of Archaeology], *Protokoly Turkestanskogo kruzhka ljubitelej arkheologii*, II, Tashkent, 1896-1897, 11 p.; G.N. Chabrov, *Istorija...*, *op. cit.* (note 36), p. 9, 39, 40, 59; *Idem, Chastnoe kollekcionerstvo dorevoljucionnogo Turkestana (1865-1917)* [Private Collecting in Pre-Revolutionary Turkestan], a manuscript, CGA RUz, F. R-2681, cat. 1, f. 100, p. 8, 18; B.V. Lunin, *Istoriografija obshchestvennykh nauk v Uzbekistane. Bio-bibliograficheskie ocherki* [Historiography of Social Sciences in Uzbekistan. A Bio-Bibliographical Survey], Tashkent, 1974, p. 120, 142, 172, 193, 200, 263, 278, 279, 282; *Idem, Srednjaja Azija v nauchnom nasledii otechestvennogo vostokovedenija. Istoriograficheskij ocherk* [Central Asia in the Scientific Heritage of Russian Oriental Studies. A Historiographical Survey], Tashkent, 1969, p. 48; N.S. Sadykova, *op. cit.* (note 113), p. 34-35, 40.

[160]S.P. Rusejkina, *loc. cit.* (note 99), p. 38.

[161]V.A. Prishchepova, *op.cit* (note 71), p. 83-110.

[162]*Turkestanskij Al'bom*, Chast' istoricheskaja, [A Turkestan Album. Historical Part], Tashkent, 1871-1872: quoted from G.N. Chabrov, *Istorija...*, *op.cit* (note 36).

[163]B.N. Kastal'skij, *Bija-najmanskie ossuarii [The Ossuaries of Biya-Naiman]*, Samarkand, 1908, 36 p. (reprinted from *Protokoly Turkestanskogo kruzhka ljubitelej arkheologii*, XIII, Tashkent, 1909, p. 1-36).

[164]CGA RUz, F. I-71, cat. 1, file 22a, p. 64.

[165]S.M. Dudin, "K voprosu o tekhnike izgatovlenija izrazcovykh mozaik Srednej Azii [On the Technique of Manufacturing Tile Mosaics in Central Asia]", *Izvestija Rossijskoj Akademii istorii material'noj kul'tury* [Proceedings of the Russian Academy for the History of Material Culture], vol. IV, Leningrad, 1925, p. 183-204.

[166]S.M. Dudin, "Sredneaziatskie kovry [Central Asian Carpets]", *Stolica i usad'ba* [The Capital and the Estate], Petrograd, 1916, N° 2; *Idem*, "Kovrovye izdelija Srednej Azii [Central Asian Carpets]", *Sbornik Muzeja antropologii i etnografii AN SSSR* [Collected Papers of the Museum of Anthropology and Ethnography, the Academy of Sciences of the USSR], Vol. VII, Leningrad, 1928, p. 71-158.

[167]S.M. Dudin, "Sobranie arkheologicheskikh kollekcij i arkheologich-

eskikh materialov preimushchestvenno po ornamentike narodnostej, nasel-jajushchikh Srednjuju Aziju, S.M.Dudina [S.M. Dudin's Collection of Archaeological Materials, Chiefly Connected with the Ornamental Arts of the Peoples Inhabiting Central Asia]", *Izvestija Imperatorskoj arkheo-logicheskoj komissii* [Proceedings of the Imperial Archaeological Committee], Saint-Petersburg, 1907. Pribavlenie k vypusku 21-mu [Addenda to Vol. 21]; *Idem*, "Ornamentika i sovremennoe sostojanie starinnykh Samarkandskikh mechetej [Ornaments and the Present State of Old Samarkand Mosques]", *ibidem*, Vol. 6, Saint-Petersburg, 1910, p. 49-73.

[168] *Idem*, "Kirgizskij ornament [The Kirghiz Ornament]", *Vostok*, vyp. V, Moscow-Leningrad, 1925, p. 120-172.

[169] B.V. Lunin, *Istoriografija...*, *op. cit.* (note 159), p. 172.

[170] S.M. Dudin, "Rez'ba po derevu u kirgiz [The Kirghiz Wood-Carving]", *Zodchij* [The Architect], Saint-Petersburg, 1901, N° 10.

[171] S.M. Dudin, "Khudozhestvennaja promyshlennost' turkmen i sar-tov (Doklad S.M. Dudina 16 fevralja 1902 g. v Obshchestve pooshchreni-ja Khudozhestv) [Artistic Handicrafts of the Turkmen and the Sarts. A report delivered by S.M. Dudin on the 16th February, 1902 to the Society for The Promotion of Arts]", *Zakaspijskoe obozrenie* [The Trans-Caspian Review], 1902, N° 57; *Idem*, "Otchet o rabotakh v mavzolejakh Shakh-Zinda v Samarkande" [A Report on the Works at the Mausoleums of Shah-i Zindah in Samarkand], *Izvestija Russkogo komiteta dlja izuchenija Srednej i Vostochnoj Azii v istoricheskom, arkheologicheskom, lingvistich-eskom i etnograficheskom otnoshenijakh* [Proceedings of the Russian Committee for the study of Central and Eastern Asia with regard to Historical, Linguistic and Ethnographical Aspects], Saint-Petersburg, 1906, N° 6, p. 26-34.

[172] S.M. Dudin, "Khudozhestvennaja promyshlennost'...", *loc. cit.* (note 171).

[173] N.F. Burdukov, *Gonchornye izdelija Srednej Azii* [Central Asian Pottery], Saint-Petersburg, 1904, XXIV p., XXII tabl.

[174] N. Burdukov, *Kovrovoe proizvodstvo Zakaspijskogo kraja i Kavkaza i zavisimost' ego ot rastitel'nykh krasok, privozimykh iz Persii* [Carpet Production of the Trans-Caspian Region and Its Dependence on Vegetable Pigments Imported from Persia], 1903, 17 p.; *Idem, Ukazatel' k kovram,*

vystavlennym na istoricheskoj vystavke v Muzee uchilishcha barona Shtiglica [A Catalogue of the Carpets Presented in the Historical Exhibition at the Museum of Baron Stiglitz' Art School], Saint-Petersburg, 1904. For information bout N.F. Burdukov's collection see: N. Kondakov, "Sobranie vostochnykh kovrov N.F. Burdukova [N.F. Burdukov's Collection of Oriental Carpets]", *Stolica i usad'ba* [The Capital and the Estate], 1916, N° 50.

[175]40 carpets published in this book were exhibited in 1902 at the Handicrafts Exhibition in the Tauric Palace and were later donated to the Museum of Alexander III (later the Russian Museum). Today 38 items of Bogolyubov's collection are listed in the catalogues of the State Museum of Ethnography in Saint-Petersburg (collection 87): S.P. Rusejkina, *loc.cit.* (note 99), p. 76.

[176]A.A. Bogoljubov, *Kovrovye izdelija Srednej Azii. Iz sobranija, sostavlennogo A.A. Bogoljubovym* [Central Asian Carpets from the Collection of A.A. Bogoljubov], Vol. I and II, Saint-Petersburg, 1908-1909, 44 p.

[177]N.I. Veselovskij, "Recenzija na al'bom Bogoljubova [Review of the Album Edited by Bogoljubov]", *Zapiski vostochnogo otdelenija rossijskogo arkheologicheskogo obshchestva* [Proceeding of the Oriental Department of the Russian Archaeological Society], t. XX, Saint-Petersburg, 1911, p. 89-93; A.A. Semenov, "Kovry...", *loc. cit.* (note 97).

[178]A.A. Fal'kerzam, *loc.cit.* (note 72).

[179]H. Moser, *Catalogue des collections ethnologiques rapportées de l'Asie centrale*, Neuchâtel, Impr. de la Société typographique, 1886; *Collection Henri Moser-Charlottenfels: armes et armures orientales*, Leipzig, K.W. Hiersemann, 1912; R. von Pfaff, "Henri Moser-Charlottenfels und seine Orientalische Sammlung", *Sonderdruck aus Schaffhauser Beiträge zur Geschichte*, 62, 1985, p. 117-156.

[180]E. de Zichy, *Voyage au Caucase et en Asie centrale. La migration de la race hongroise*. La description des collections par les docteurs Jean Jancö et Bela de Posta, vol. I, Budapest, Gustave Ranschburg Libraire-Editeur, 1897.

[181]E. Blochet, "Les Inscriptions de Samarkand. (I. Le Goûr-i-Mîr, ou Tombeau de Tamerlan, épitaphes de Timoûr et de plusieurs princes timoûrides)", Paris, E. Leroux, 1897, 42 p. (Extr. de la *Revue archéologique*).

[182] All of the objects in Ujfalvy's collection were depicted in tables of high artistic merit, compiled by V. Schmidt. Ch.-E. Ujfalvy, *Expédition...*, *op.cit.* (note 50), t. 5. *Atlas des étoffes, bijoux, aiguières, émaux, etc. de l'Asie centrale*, 1880, 23 pl. en noir gr. par B. Schmidt; t. 6. *Atlas archéologique des antiquités finno-ougriennes et altaïques de la Russie, de la Sibérie et du Turkestan*, 1880, 23 pl. gr. par B. Schmidt.

[183] Ch.-E. Ujfalvy, *L'Art des cuivres anciens au Cachemire et au Petit Thibet*, Paris, 1883.

[184] Mirza Bukhari, "Pis'ma iz Samarkanda [A Letter from Samarkand]", *Turkestanskaja tuzemnaja gazeta* [The Turkestanian Local Newspaper], N° 19, 14.05.1888.

[185] E.g. about Mirza Bukhari' collection: *Turkestanskie Vedomosti* [The Turkestanian News], 1888, N° 12, N° 19.

[186] The catalogue was ready by the late 1920s. Today it is preserved in the Institute for Oriental Studies of the Academy of Sciences of Uzbekistan. See: Sh. Vahidov, A. Erkinov, "Le fihrist (catalogue) de la bibliothèque de Sadr-i Ziyâ: une image de la vie intellectuelle dans le Mavarannahr (fin XIXe-début XXe siècles)", *Cahiers d'Asie centrale*, n° 7, 1999, p. 141-163.

[187] Riza-Kuli-Mirza, *Kratkij ocherk Amudar'inskoj oblasti* [A Short Description of the Amu-Darya District], Saint-Petersburg, 1875, 43 p.; P.P. Semenov, *Istorija poluvekovoj dejatel'nosti Imperatorskogo Russkogo geograficheskogo obshchestva. 1845-1895* [A History of Half a Century of the Activities of the Imperial Russian Geographical Society. 1845-1895], ch. 2, Saint-Petersburg, 1896, p. 811-812.

[188] 1870s: Grand Duke N.K. Romanov. 1880s: Prince Trubetskoy, Count A.A. Polovtsev. 1890s: Count A.A. Bobrinsky; Count E.E. Ukhtomsky. 1900s: Baron A.A. Falkersam.

[189] 1860s: Head of the Zarafshan District, General-Major A.K. Abramov; General L.F. Ballyuzek; Colonel Ch. Valikhanov; General N.N. Golovachev; Governor-General K.P. von Kaufmann; General N.A. Kryzhanovsky; Colonel A.A. Kushakevich; Governor-General M.G. Chernyaev. 1870s: Major Borzenkov; military engineer General G.A. Kolpakovsky; participant in the Khivan campaign of 1873 D.M. Rezvoi; military band master A.F. Eichhorn. 1880s: Colonel A.G. Arendorenko; Colonel M. Alikhanov-Avarsky; General N.I. Grodekov; Colonel

Kazantsev; General A.V. Komarov; the Russian consul in Kashgar General
N.F. Petrovsky; Lieutenant-General of the Engineers I.T. Poslavsky.
1890s: Lieutenant-Colonel L.S. Barszscewski; Russian political agent in
Bukhara V.I. Ignatyev; Head of the Perovsk District, V.A. Kallaur; the
diplomat working for the administration of the Trans-Caspian Region,
A.D. Kalmykov; the Russian political agent in Bukhara, Ja.Ja. Lutsh; Head
of the Lepsinsk District, K.N. de Lazari; Admiral K.N.Pos'et. 1900s: Head
of the Trans-Caspian Region, General A.A. Bogolyubov; General S.M.
Dukhovskoy; the military governor of the Samarkand Region, the
Orientalist, N.S. Lykoshin; General Mishchenko. 1910s: General A.S.
Galkin; Colonel G.A. Nasibianc; Colonel (geologist) G.A. Shpilko.

[190] 1870s: official for special assignments: B.N. Kastalsky; druggist I.I.
Krause; excise official of the Zerafshan District, D.O. Petrov-Borzna; offi-
cial for special assignments, Ju.D. Juzhakov. 1880s: lawyer Bolotin; Osh
District J.P. D.M. Gramenitsky; N.A. Kashtalinsky, manager of the state
manor in Murgab. 1890s: Engineer M.F. Mauer; state official S.M.
Nizhansky; photographer S.F. Nikolai; state official M.V. Stolyariov.
1900s: state official N.F. Burdukov; state official A.I. Dobrosmyslov; doc-
tor in the Samarkand Region K.E. Ostrovskikh; inspector of taxes P.E.
Ostrovskikh. 1910s: state official J.-A. Castagné; state official F.F.
Popelov; antique-dealer E.I. Aleksander; mining engineer I.N. Glushkov;
I.N. Rachinsky; forester V.D. Pel'c; V. Emme.

[191] In this group, in which the scholars of Saint-Petersburg coming to
Turkestan on scientific missions obviously prevail, we find the
Turkestanian officials, who belonged to the researchers because of their
education and the character of their professional activity rather than their
formal posts, if we take into consideration the fact that there was no real
research infrastructure in Turkestan. 1840s: researcher (Orientalist) N.V.
Khanykov (Saint-Petersburg). 1850s: researcher (Orientalist) P.I. Lerch
(Saint-Petersburg); researcher (Orientalist) V.V. Velyaminov-Zernov
(Saint-Petersburg); researcher (Orientalist) V.V. Grigoryev (Saint-
Petersburg); researcher (naturalist) L.I. Schrenck (Saint-Petersburg).
1860s: official for special assignments and the researcher (geologist) D.L.
Ivanov (Saint-Petersburg). 1870s: official for special assignments and
researcher (naturalist) A.I. Vil'kens (Tashkent); official for special assign-
ments and researcher (Orientalist) A.L. Kun (Saint-Petersburg); official
and researcher (naturalist) N.A. Mayev (Tashkent); official and researcher
(Orientalist) N.P. Ostroumov (Tashkent); official and researcher (natural-

ist) V.F. Oshanin (Tashkent); official for special assignments and researcher (Orientalist) N.N. Pantusov (Tashkent); the official for special assignments and researcher (Orientalist) M.N. Rostislavov (Samarkand); researcher (naturalist) O.A. Fedchenko (Saint-Petersburg); researcher (botanist) S.M. Smirnov (Saint-Petersburg). 1880s: researcher (Orientalist) V.V. Bartold (Saint-Petersburg); researcher (Orientalist) N.I. Veselovsky (Saint-Petersburg); official for special assignments and researcher (Orientalist) E.F. Kal' (Saint-Petersburg). 1890s: official for special assignments and researcher (Orientalist) M.S. Andreyev (Tashkent); official and researcher (self-taught Orientalist) V.L. Vyatkin (Samarkand); researcher (Orientalist) V.A. Zhukovsky (Saint-Petersburg); official and researcher (naturalist) V.P. Nalivkin (Tashkent); researcher (naturalist) I.E. Regel (Saint-Petersburg); researcher (naturalist) G.E. Grumm-Grzhymailo (Saint-Petersburg). 1900s: official and researcher (Orientalist) A.A. Semenov (Tashkent); researcher (geologist) Ja.S. Edelstein. 1910s: official and researcher (Orientalist) M.F. Gavrilov (Tashkent); researcher (Orientalist) V.A. Ivanov (Saint-Petersburg); researcher (entomologist) A.K. Golbek; researcher (orientalist) K.V. Shchennikov (Saint-Petersburg).

[192] 1870s: writer N.N. Karazin; 1880s: official for special assignments and writer Colonel V.V. Krestovsky.

[193] 1860s: painter V.V. Vereshchagin; 1900s: painters S.M. Dudin, L.E. Dmitriev-Kavkazsky, A. Voronina-Utkina, B.F. Romberg, N.N. Shcherbina-Kramarenko, A.A. Karelin, Kotorbinsky (part of their collections are at the Kunstkamera: Nr. 2519 for Voronina-Utkina, Nr. 2265 for Romberg and Nr. 1487 for Sherbina-Kramarenko): V.A. Prishchepova, *op.cit.* (note 71), p. 52, 54, 67-68).

[194] See: S. Gorshenina, B. Chukhovich, *Orientalism of the Russian School of Art* (forthcoming).

[195] The vast majority of western expeditions went through Russian Turkestan and were destined for China, the Pamirs or Tibet where the largest collections, both naturalist and especially historical and cultural (archaeological objects, frescos, manuscripts, coins) were made. In particular, for the Chinese Turkestan we should not forget to mention the collections of S.A. Hedin, a Swede, 1885-1933; H. Dauvergne, a Frenchman, 1888-1889; G. Macarthney, a Scot, 1890-1918; J.-L. Dutreuil de Rhins and F. Grenard, Frenchmen, 1891; J.F. Duthie, an Englishman, 1893-1895; A.W. Alcock, an Englishman, 1895; A. Stein, an Englishman, 1900-1930;

A. Grünwedel, 1902-1907, and T. Bartus, 1902-1907, G. Huth, 1902, and A. von Le Coq, 1904-1907, Germans; C.G.E. Mannerheim, Russian, of Finnish origin, 1906-1908; P. Pelliot, a Frenchman, 1906-1909; L. Warner, an American, 1903, 1923, 1925. For Afghanistan and the Pamirs: collections of Ch. Masson, an Englishman (1840s); H.W. Bellew, an Englishman, 1872-1874; F. Stoliczka and L. James Trotter, 1870, 1874; and the Treasure of the Oxus, 1877. See: R.A. Hoernle, "Collection of antiques from Central Asia", *Journal of the Asiatic Society of Bombay*, v. 68, 1899, N° 1; P. Hopkirk, *Foreign devils on the Silk Road*, London, J. Murray, 1980; *idem, Trespassers on the Roof of the World*, London, J. Murray, 1982; A. Baud, Ph. Forêt, S. Gorshenina, *La Haute-Asie telle qu'ils l'ont vue. Explorateurs et scientifiques de 1820 à 1940*, Genève, Olizane, 2003.

[196]For details see: S. Gorshenina, *Explorateurs en Asie centrale, op. cit.* (note 19), p. 85-88.

[197]Gerlach, a German with a group of tourists who came to Samarkand in April-May of 1898; an Englishman registered as *"Vul'rich Peterson"*, who in 1897 and 1898, together with Captain Benett, accompanied a group of 30 persons, who lived in a railway carriage during their journey: S. Gorshenina, *Explorateurs en Asie centrale, op. cit.* (note 19), p. 88.

[198]Thus, in the period from 7th June to 26th July, 1913 a party of schoolchildren on a excursion from the Warsaw Educational District visited Turkestan following the route: Warsaw – Moscow – Nizhny Novgorod – Samara – Orenburg – the Aral Sea Station – Tashkent – Golodnaya Step' Station – Kokand – Andijan – Samarkand – Bukhara – Bayram-Ali – Iolotan' Station – Ashkhabad – Krasnovodsk – Baku – Mineralnye Vody – Novorossiysk – Sebastopol – Kiev – Warsaw. CGA RUz, F. I-3, cat., 1, f. 347, p. 283.

[199]F. Desmousseaux de Givre went on a trip to Turkestan with his friends on graduating from university in 1908: F. Desmousseaux de Givre, *De Paris en Asie centrale en voyage de vacances, souvenirs et impressions*, Paris, éd. Marcel Rivière, 1908.

[200]Germans: *"Godefrua Merjabakher"*, 1892; *"Kurt Bekk"*, 1898. Frenchmen: Louis d'Estaing D'Estampes, 1890; Gaston Chasseloup Laubat, 1890. *"Frank Vincent"*, an American, 1890, 1892; *"Geger"*, an Austrian, 1890; *"Saturnino Gimenes Ekrikh"*, a Spaniard, 1892; Revilliod, a Swiss, 1892. Prohibition of unauthorized archaeological exca-

vations applied to Russian subjects as well, which was mentioned in the first circular - prohibiting archaeological research - issued by K.P. von Kaufmann, Chief of Turkestan Region, and published in 1871 by the newspaper *Turkestanskie Vedomosti* [The Turkestanian News].

[201] Archives Nationales de France, Archives du Ministère des Affaires étrangères, Archives du Ministère de la défense (Service historique de l'Armée de Terre), Bibliothèque Nationale de France (Départements des manuscrits, des cartes et plans, des estampes et de la photographie).

[202] Excluding 200,000 or 150,000 prisoners of war and 300-350 deported Austro-Hungarians and Germans mentioned by A.M. Matveev. See: A.M. Matveev, *Uchastie zarubezhnykh vykhodcev v ekonomicheskoj i social'no-politicheskoj zhizni dorevoljucionnogo i sovetskogo Turkestana (1914-1920)*, [Participation of Foreigners in the Economic, Social and Political Life of Pre-Revolutionary and Soviet Turkestan.], doctoral thesis, Tashkent, 1975, 354 p.; S. Gorshenina, *Explorateurs en Asie centrale, op. cit.* (note 19), p. 85-88.

[203] L. Aubain, "La Russie à l'exposition universelle de 1889", *Cahiers du monde russe et soviétique*, 1996, XXXVII (3), p. 357, 358; G.N. Chabrov, "Vystavochnaja rabota v dorevoljucionnom Turkestane [Exhibition in of Pre-Revolutionary Turkestan]", *Trudy muzeja istorii UzSSR* [Transactions of the Museum of History of the Uzbek SSR], Vol. 3, Tashkent, 1956, p. 118-138; *Idem*, "Turkestan na vserossijskikh i vsemirnykh vystavkakh [Turkestan at All-Russian and International Exhibitions]", *Trudy Sredneaziatskogo Gosudarstvennogo Universiteta* [Proceedings of the Central Asian State University], Vol. 142, Tashkent, 1958, p. 41-60.

[204] A.M. Matveev, *op. cit.* (note 202); *Idem*, "Uchastie zarubezhnykh vykhodcev v obshchestvenno-politicheskoj zhizni Turkestana v marte-sentjabre 1917 [Participation of Foreigners in the Social and Political Life of Turkestan in March-September 1917]", *Materialy po istorii i arkheologii Srednej Azii* [Materials for the Study of History and Archaeology of Central Asia], t. 473, Tashkentskij gosudarstvennyj Universitet [Tashkent State University], 1974, p. 78-79.

[205] A.M. Matveev based his analysis upon: Girshfel'd, Galkin, *Voenno-statisticheskoe opisanie Khorezmijskogo oazisa* [Military Statistics of the Khwaresmian Oasis], ch. 2, Tashkent, 1903; *Obzor Semirechenkoj oblasti za 1909 g.* [A Survey of the Semirechye Region for the Year, 1909], Verny,

1911; *Obzor Samarkanskoj oblasti za 1910 g.* [A Survey of the Samarkand Region for the Year, 1910], Samarkand, 1912, pr. N° 3; *Obzor Syr-dar'inskoj oblasti za 1909 g.* [A Survey of the Syr-Darya Region for the Year, 1909], Tashkent, 1911; *Statisticheskij obzor Ferganskoj oblasti za 1910 g.* [A Statistical Survey of the Ferghana Region for the Year, 1910], Skobelev, 1912; *Obzor Zakaspijskoj oblasti za 1911 g.* [A Survey of the Trans-Caspian Region for the Year, 1911], Ashkhabad, 1915; S.R. Konopka, *Turkestanskijj kraj* [The Province of Turkestan], 2 izd., Tashkent, 1912; *Perepis' naselenija v Turkestanskoj respublike (1920 g.)* [Census of the Population in the Turkestan Republic (1920)], ch. 1, n° 1, *Poselennye itogi Turkestanskoj oblasti* [Statistics on the Settlements in the Turkestan Region], Tashkent, 1922; vyp. 2, *Poselennye itogi Amu-dar'inkoj oblasti* [Statistics on the Settlements in the Amu-Darya Region], Tashkent, 1923; Vol. 4, *Sel'skoe naselenie Ferganskoj oblasti po materialam peripisi 1917 g.* [Rural Population of the Ferghana Region based on the Census of 1917], Tashkent, 1924; Vol. 5, *Poselennye itogi Samarkanskoj oblasti* [Statistics on the Settlements in the Samarkand Region], Tashkent, 1924; *Materialy po rajonirovaniju Srednej Azii* [Materials for the Administrative Division of Central Asia], Book. 1, *Territorija i naselenie Bukhary i Khorezma* [The Territory and the population of Bukhara and Khwaresm], Pt. 1, Bukhara, Tashkent, 1926; Pt. 2. *Khorezm*, Tashkent, 1926; *Statisticheskij ezhegodnik Turkestanskoj respubliki 1917-1923 gg*, [Statistical Yearbook of the Turkestan Republic 1917-1923] t. 1, Tashkent, 1924; O.A. Sukhareva, *K istorii gorodov Bukharskogo khanstva (Istoriko- etnografîcheskie ocherki)* [The History of the Cities of the Bukharan Khanate (Historical and Ethnographical Essays)], Tashkent, 1958, etc.

[206] 1820s: J.B. Fraser, a Scot, 1821-1822. 1870s: A.E. Brehm, naturalist, zoologist with O. Finsch and an officer, Count "*G.K. Val'dburg-Cejl'*", Germans, 1876; J. Martin, a Frenchmen, topographer, geologist and member of the Geographical Society of Paris, 1879-1886, 1889-1892; F.X. von Schwarz, a German naturalist and astronomer, 1874-early 1880s; Ch.-E. Ujfalvy de Mezö Kövesd, a Hungarian and a Frenchmen, 1876-1877, 1879, 1881. 1880s: G. Bonvalot, a French geographer and explorer, trips in 1880, 1882, 1886-1887, 1889; G. Capus, of Luxembourg, naturalist, explorer, 1882, 1886-1887; H. Lansdell, an Englishman, 1884. 1890s: H.-R. d'Allemagne, a French archivist and paleographer at the Bibliothèque de l'Arsenal, 1898, 1907; J. Chaffanjon, a French explorer, 1894-1895; P. Labbe, a French linguist and ethnologist, 1897; the Danes, naturalist A.

Hjuler and botanist, Master Assistant at the Higher School in Randers, O. Paulsen, 1896-1897, 1898-1899 (Olufsen's expeditions); E. de Poncins, a French naturalist, 1893-1894; W.R. Rickmers, a German explorer, 1896, 1898, 1906, 1907, 1908, 1913, 1928 (together with A. von Krafft, 1898, M.H. von Friederichsen, 1902, G. Merzbacher, 1902-1903, K. Leuchs, A. Lorenz, 1906, Germans, A.D.M. Carruthers, an Englishman, 1907); "*K. Rosst*", an English naturalist, 1898; C. Saaro, a German naturalist, 1891-1897. 1900s: J. Brocherel, an Italian anthropologist, 1900; R. Pumpelly, an American geographer and geologist, with W.M. Davis, geologist, an expert in fluvial erosion, Professor of Geology at Harvard and E. Huntington, Research Assistant at the Carnegie Institution, 1903-1904; "*K.R. Goldovitch Stal' fon Golshtein*", "*K. fon Menzenkampf*", "*E. Volf*", Finns, 1912-1913.

[207] J.M.A. de Cuverville, a Frenchman, cavalryman, admiral, senator of Finistere from 1901 to 1912, trip in 1895; O. Olufsen, lieutenant, Dane, 1896-1897, 1898-1899; H. de Bouillane de Lacoste, a Frenchman, 1906.

[208] E.g. in France, such missions were financed by the French Ministries of Foreign Affairs, of Public Education, of Colonies, of Labour, of Public Works, of Agriculture, of Trade and Sea Trade. At the same time, it was not unusual that the state shared expenses with private persons. Thus, J. Chaffanjon's expedition in 1894-1895 was financed by the Ministry of Public Education and by L. Mangini; the expedition of O. Olufsen, a Dane, in 1897-1897 and in 1898-1899 was financed by the Danish Parliament, the Carlsberg Foundation (Danish Consul A. Nissen in Rostov-on-the-Don) and the businessman P. Morck in Saint-Petersburg. The Carnegie Institution, a private foundation, financed R. Pumpelly's mission in 1903-1904.

[209] 1890s: E. Blanc, French, geographer, naturalist and an expert on the construction of railways, 1890-1892, 1894-1895; E. Masson, French, Member of *la Société de géographie de Paris*, Secretary-in Chief at *le Tribunal de commerce de Versailles*, sent - in 1892 - to Turkestan by the Chamber of Commerce of Lyon in view of the Colonial Exhibition of 1894.

[210] 1860s: H. Moser, Swiss and Russian, four journeys in 1868-1869, 1870, 1883-1884, 1889-1890. 1890s: H. Krafft, French, 1898-1899. 1900s: J.-A. Castagné, French and Russian, 1912-1921; 1930: E. Maillart, a Swiss woman, 1932, 1934, 1935.

[211] 1900s: Leon Blot, French, 1905; Samuel Salm, Swede, 1900-1914.

[212]1840s: J. Laurens, French, a trip in 1848, his works are to be seen at the Museums of Carpentras and Avignon and at the School of Fine Arts in Paris. See: Mme Hommaire de Hell: *Les Steppes de la mer Caspienne, voyage dans la Russie méridionale*, Paris, Didier, 1868 (2nd ed.), X, 367 p.; B. Zaleski, Pole, 1840-1850, his drawings are published in *La Vie des steppes kirghizes*, Paris, 1865; 1880s: A. Pepin, French, a trip in 1886-1887, see his drawings in: G. Bonvalot, *Du Caucase aux Indes à travers le Pamir. Ouvrage orné de 250 dessins par A. Pepin avec une carte d'itinéraire du voyage*, Paris, E. Plon, Nourrit et C°, 1889; L. Gay, landscape-painter and photographer, French, 1894-1895.

[213]M. Hordet, French, 1885-1892; P. Nadar, French, 1890.

[214]1890: E.N. Adler, 1897; 1900: E. Hindamian, 1912 (?).

[215]E. Schuyler, American, 1873.

[216]Count A. de La Baume Pluvinel, a Frenchman, 1887; Marquis de E.C. Croizier, a Frenchman, 1890 (?); Viscount E. de Poncins, a Frenchman, 1893-1894; Count E. de Zichy, an Austro-Hungarian, 1898; Roman Prince S. Borghese, 1900; Baron *"K.R.Goldovitch Stal' fon Golshtein"*, Finn, 1912-1913.

[217]A.A. Semenov, "Nechto...", *loc. cit.* (note 44), p. 145.

[218]One of the largest collections of "girikhs" was that of Mîrzâ Barat Mullâ Kasymov. About "girikhs", see L.I. Rempel', *Arkhitekturnyj ornament Uzbekistana. Istorija razvitija i teorija postroenija* [Architectural Ornaments of Uzbekistan. Its Historical Development and Theoretical Structure], Tashkent, 1961, p. 6-18.

[219]Mak-Gakhan, *Voennye dejstvija na Oksuse i padenie Khivy*, Per. s ang., Moscow, 1875 [J.A. MacGahan, *Campaigning on the Oxus and the fall of Khiva*, by J.A. MacGahan, correspondent of the 'New York Herald', New York, Harper & Brothers, 1874, X, 438 p.]

[220]P. Uvarova, "Poezdka v Tashkent...", *loc. cit.* (note 43), p. 15.

[221]H. Moser, *oc. cit.* (note 47), p. 160; G.N. Chabrov, "Uzbeki-arkheologi dorevoljucionnogo Uzbekistana [Uzbek Archaeologists of Pre-Revolutionary Uzbekistan]", *Zvezda Vostoka* [*The Star of the Orient*], 1957, N° 1, p. 144-146.

[222]Arif-Khodja Arifkhodjinov, Colonel Djurabek, Mukhitdin-Khodja Khakim Khodja Ishanov, the brothers Seid Kari and Seid Karim Seid Azimbaev, Kutlu-Khajdar Arslanov, Adul-Kasymkhan Bakykhan, Bek

Kulybek Jakkubekov, Allakulibek Djuravekov, A.A. Divaev, Ishan-khodja Makhmudkhodjin, Mîrzâ Abdullah Issamukhammadov, Mulla-Alim Abulkasymov, Mulla Mujadut Akhtajmov. See: *Protokoly Turkestanskogo kruzhka ljubitelej arkheologii* [Proceedings of the Turkestanian Circle of Friends of Archaeology], god I-XX, Tashkent, 1896-1917.

[223]N.I. Veselovsky, *loc. cit.* (note 61), p. 112.

[224]B.V. Lunin, "Uzbekskij arkheolog-ljubitel' i sobiratel' drevnostej Akram-Palvan Askarov [Uzbek Amateur Archaeologist and Collector of Antiques Akram-Palvan Askarov]", *Izvestija Akademii nauk UzSSR* [Proceedings of the Academy of Sciences of the USSR], Serija Obshchestvennykh nauk, Tashkent, 1960, N° 6, p. 66-76; *Idem*, "O numizmaticheskoj kollekcii uzbekskogo sobiratelja drevnostej Akrama Askarova (po arkhivnym dannym) [On the Numismatical Collection of the Uzbek Collector of Antiques, Akram Askaron (according to Archive Documents)]", *Istorija material'noj kul'tury Uzbekistana* [A History of the Material Culture of Uzbekistan], Tashkent, 1964, Vol. V, p. 233-244.

[225]B.V. Lunin, "Samarkandskij ljubitel' [...] Mirza Bukhari", *loc. cit.* (note 120), p. 32-40.

[226]G. Astanova, R. Bajtullaev, "Master kalligrafii [A Master of Calligraphy]", *Leninskij put'* [The Leninist Way], 1977, 14.09.

[227]V.A. Prishchepova, *op.cit.* (note 71), p. 63.

[228]A.L. Kun, "Poezdka po Khivinskomu khanstvu v 1873 godu [A Trip to the Khiva Khanate]", *Izvestija Imperatorskogo russkogo geograficheskogo obshchestva* [Proceedings of the Imperial Russian Geographical Society], Saint-Petersburg, 1874, Vol. X, Pt. 2, p. 47-58; V.V. Stasov, "Tron...", *loc. cit.* (note 87); A. Bobrinskij, *Ornament gornykh tadzhikov Darvaza. Nagornaja Bukhara [Ornaments of the Mountain Tajiks of Darvaz. Highland Bukhara]*, Moscow, 1900; S.M. Dudin, "Khudozhestvennaja promyshlennost' turkmen...", *loc. cit.* (note 171); A.A. Polovtsev, "Zametki o musul'manskom iskusstve (po proizvedenijam v Muzee Shtiglica [Notes on Moslem Art (based on the works at the Stiglitz' Museum)]", *Starye gody* [The Old Years], 1913, oktjabr'; S.P. Rusejkina, *loc. cit.* (note 99), p. 46, 49, 50. Ethnographic collections are also treated in some publications in the series *Sbornik Muzeja antropologii i etnografii.* T. XVII, 1957, T. XLIII, 1989, etc, as well as in the catalogues of the Museum of Anthropology and Ethnography (Kunstkamera).

[229] S.P. Rusejkina, *loc. cit.* (note 99), p. 76.

[230] Museum of Anthropology and Ethnography of the Russian Academy of Sciences (Kunstkamera, Saint-Petersburg), collections Nr. 2019, 2020, 2137, 2804: S.P. Rusejkina, *loc. cit.* (note 99), p. 49.

[231] Museum of Anthropology and Ethnography (Kunstkamera), collection Nr. 1710: S.P. Rusejkina, *loc. cit.* (note 99), p. 80.

[232] These collections were donated to the Museum of Anthropology and Ethnography (Kunstkamera, Nr. 2 and 52) in 1881 but have now disappeared. S.P. Rusejkina, *loc. cit.* (note 99), p. 82; V.A. Prishchepova, *op.cit.* (note 71), p. 28.

[233] V.A. Prishchepova, *op.cit.* (note 71), p. 37-38.

[234] Mîrzâ Bukhari, who visited Kharkov, Moscow and Saint-Petersburg in 1897, published his notes in the newspaper *Turkestan vilojating gazetasi*, 1888, N° 4-7; later they were reprinted in: N.P. Ostroumov, *Sarty, Etnograficheskie Materialy (Obshchij ocherk)* [The Sarts, Ethnographical Materials. A General Survey], Tashkent, 1908, p. 192-200.

[235] O.V. Maslova, *op. cit.* (note 20), 5 vols, Tashkent, 1955-1971; S. Gorshenina, *La route de Samarcande: l'Asie centrale dans l'objectif des voyageurs d'autrefois*, Catalogue de l'exposition photographique au Musée d'ethnographie de Genève, Genève, Olizane, 2000, 260 p.; S. Gorshenina, *Explorateurs en Asie centrale, op. cit.* (note 19).

[236] The predecessors of the Tashkent Museum were a small collection of rock minerals, medicinal plants and coins collected by the Tashkent Chemical Laboratory, and a small museum of sericulture organized by V.F. Oshanin at the School for Sericulture: *Turkestanskie Vedomosti [The Turkestanian News]*, 1884, N° 1; G.N. Chabrov, *Istorija..., op. cit.* (note 36), p. 23.

[237] V.S. Minosjanc, "K istorii komplektovanija archeologicheskogo fonda Muzeja istorii narodov Uzbekistana (1876-1917) [On the History of the Archaeological Funds of the Museum of the Peoples of Uzbekistan (1876-1917)]", *Vremen svjazujushchaja nit' (po materialam muzejnykh fondov* [The Thread Connecting Times (based on materials from museum collections)], Tashkent, 1992, p. 3.

[238] *Trudy VII Arkheologicheskogo S'ezda v Jaroslavle. 1887 god,* pod. red. Grafini Uvarovoj, vol. 2, Moscow, 1891. Prilozhenie k dokladu Uvarovoj [Proceedings of the 7th Archaeological Congress in Yaroslavl.

1887. Ed. by Countess Uvarova. Vol. 2. Appendix to Uvarova's report]. See also *Opisanie numizmaticheskoj kollekcii Tashkentskogo muzeja i Turkestanskogo arkheologicheskogo kruzhka, sostavitel' I.I. Trofimov.* Prilozhenie k PTKLA, god 6, 1901 [Description of the numismatical collection of the Museum of Tashkent and of the Turkestanian Archaeological Circle, by Trofimov].

[239]E. Markov, *op. cit.* (note 74), t. I, p. 103.

[240]J. Chaffanjon, "Rapport sur une mission scientifique dans l'Asie centrale et la Sibérie" *in Nouvelles archives des missions scientifiques et littéraires,* Paris, Impr. nationale, 1899, 9, p. 55. Here are some more typical examples of the universality of European expeditions to Central Asia. Three expeditions by Ch.-E. Ujfalvy: exploration of flora and fauna, archaeological excavations, studies on geography, urbanistics, anthropology and ethnography. J.L. Dutreuil de Rhins et F. Grenard: research into geology, botany, astronomy, meteorology, history, linguistics, geography and archaeology. E. Blanc was interested in geography, flora and fauna, irrigation archaeology, ethnography, anthropology, railway constructions, cartography and architecture; P. Gault: ethnography, natural sciences, urbanism and politics; J. Chaffanjon: geography, archaeology, anthropology, ethnography, zoology, botany, geology and mineralogy; J.A. Castagné's publications were dedicated to archaeology, hydrology, speleology, folklore, religious beliefs, architecture and politics. With regard to the Russian researchers, it is worth mentioning the botanical, mineralogical, entomological, fossil, archaeological and numismatical collections made by A.E. Regel on his journey to the Pamirs and the Trans-Caspian Region, and then to Merv and Eastern Bukhara, 1881, 1884.

[241]Ch.-E. Ujfalvy, *Expédition française...*, *op. cit.* (note 50), v. 5; v. 2, p. 48, 82, 84, 87.

[242]The inventory of the numismatical collection was made be Ujfalvy himself; however, many of his identifications, as E.V. Rtveladze pointed out, to whom the author expresses her acknowledgement, are sometimes incorrect both because of discrepancies regarding certain historical facts, and because it was impossible to draw parallels with the types of coins, known at the time. Rather questionable is also Ujfalvy's way of transliterating legends of coins. For these reasons, the inventory of the collection is presented (including disputable identifications) in its original form. Silver coins: one tetradrachma of Eucratides; one dinar of Mahmud Ghaznevid,

issued in Nishapur; idem, Ghazni (416); *idem,* Ghazni (417); idem, Herat (405); dirham of Khan Hek Nalu; dirham of Khan Hek Ahmed ben Aly (obviously, Karakhanid – S.G.); dirham of Samanid Hukh ben Mansur; dirham of Timurid Sharukh; dirham of Timurid Ahmed Gurekan (after Timur the Title of Gurugan was given only to Ulugbek and Abu Said – S.G.); double dirham or Timurid Thouya Khan; double dirham of Khan Djagatap Mangou Khan; dirham of one of the Timurids (?); double dirham of Obepd Allah Bahadour (Ubeidallah - ?; 940 and s.d.); idem (944); 3 double dirhams of Abdulatif; double dirham of Abdulgazi, double dirham of Muhammad khan. See: Ch.-E. Ujfalvy, *Expédition française..., op. cit.* (note 50), v. 2, p. 82.

[243]Old Bukharan manuscripts, dated back - by the collector himself - to the 14th century [E. Blanc, "Présentation de deux manuscrits provenant de l'Asie centrale", *Bulletin du Muséum d'Histoire naturelle,* 1896, N° 4; *Idem,* "Sur deux manuscrits provenant de l'Asie centrale", *Compte rendu des séances de la Société de géographie et de la Commission centrale* (Paris), 1896], architectural ceramics, Nestorian epitaphs, photographs, ethnographical and anthropological collections, archaeological materials (over 6,000 medals, engraved stones, figurines, jewellery, coins, including Graeco-Bactrian and Indo-Scythian, which - according to E. Blanc - were mostly found on short excavations; the Soviet archaeologist, V.A. Shishkin, supposes that the coins were most probably bought from the native residents: V.A. Shishkin, *loc. cit.* [note 63], p. 38).

[244]53 cases, sent by J. Chaffanjon from Turkestan to the Botanical Gardens of the *Muséum d'histoire naturelle* (Central Asia), full of collections of animals, insects, reptiles, mammals, ethnographical objects, archaeological finds, geological specimens and some grafts. J. Chaffanjon himself wrote, in his report to the Ministry of Public Education, that the first cases he sent contained Turkestan collections: archaeological collections from the sites of Afrasiab and Paykend; fragments of mosaics and majolica from the monuments of Bukhara and Samarkand; gravestones decorated with fired clay ornamentation, supports for the Koran from Samarkand, a collection of Sart ethnic musical instruments, a collection of modern ceramics and specimens of old mosaics, a jurt and skeletons of several animals. See: French National Archives, Fond F 17 / 17270, p. 1-4.

[245]R.N. Balsiger, E.J. Kläy, *op. cit.* (note 148).

[246]H. Krafft, *A travers le Turkestan russe,* ouvrage illustré de deux cent

soixante-cinq gravures d'après les clichés de l'auteur et contenant une carte en couleurs, Paris, Hachette, 1902; N. d'Esterno, "Hommage à Hugues Krafft. Présentation de l'exposition du centenaire", Annuaire-Bulletin de la Société des amis du vieux Reims, 1984-1985, Reims, Musée-Hôtel Le Vergeur, p. 29-33.

[247] E. Fihl, *Exploring Central Asia. [...] from the Steppes to the High Pamirs 1896-1999*, 1-2 vol. (in print). See also note 288.

[248] *The Schuyler collection*, Ithaca, Cornell University Libraries N.Y., [n.d.], p. [301]-315.

[249] Among the Russian collectors, complex collections were predominant (85% general collections vs 15% specialized collections). All the Western European collections, made in central Asia, were complex (except for that of E.N. Adler). Among the Central Asian collectors the only kind of specialized collections were those of manuscripts.

[250] *Polnaja kollekcija muzykal'nykh instrumentov narodov Central'noj Azii A.F.Ejkhgorna (byvshego voennogo kapel'mejstera v Tashkente).* Katalog, [A Complete Collection of Musical Instruments of Central Asian Peoples, Made by A.F. Eichhorn (Former Military Bandmaster in Tashkent). A Catalogue], Saint-Petersburg, 1885. The passage cited is from A.F. Ejkhgorn, *Muzykal'naja fol'kloristika v Uzbekistane (pervye zapisi)* [Musical Folkloristic in Uzbekistan (the First Records)], Tashkent, 1963, p. 186-194.

[251] *Protokoly Turkestanskogo kruzhka ljubitelej arkheologii* [Proceedings of the Turkestanian Circle of Friends of Archaeology], god XII, Tashkent, 1908; V.S. Minosjanc, *loc.cit.* (note 237), p. 7.

[252] *Catalogue of Hebrew manuscripts in the collection of Elkan Nathan Adler*, Cambridge, University press, 1921, XII-228 p.; *Adler Special Manuscript Collection from the Library of the Jewish Theological Seminary: an index to the microfilm collection*, Ann Arbor, Mich., University Microfilms International, 1981.

[253] A.A. Bogoljubov, *op. cit.* (note 176, 177); reviewed in: A.A Semenov, "Kovry…", *loc. cit.* (note 97).

[254] A.A. Fal'kerzam, *loc. cit.* (note 72); A.A Semenov, "Bibliograficheskij ukazatel' po kovravym tkanjam Srednej Azii [A Bibliographical Index on Carpet Fabrics of Central Asia]", *Trudy bibliograficheskoj komissii pri SNK TSSR* [Transactions of the Bibliographical

Committee of the Soviet People's Commissars of TSSR], Vol. 1, Tashkent, 1925.

[255]G.N. Chabrov, *Chastnoe kollekcionerstvo...*, *op. cit.* (note 159), p. 17.

[256]The collections gathered in 1915-1916 are at the Museum of Anthropology and Ethnography (Kunstkamera, Nr. 2472, 2542, 2567): V.A. Prishchepova, *op.cit.* (note 71), p. 68-69. V.A. Ivanov also collected objects relating to the sedentary population of Bukhara, Shahr-i Sabz, Katta-Kurgan, Karshi, and Ferghana.

[257]The idea of a transition from complex to specialized collecting was popular among Soviet scholars. See, e.g., the works by G.N. Chabrov.

[258]A vivid picture of the character of ethnografical collections is provided in the description of the ethnographical finds of Russian and Central Asian Museums made by S.P. Rusejkina, *loc. cit.* (note 99), p. 47-85.

[259]H. Moser, *oc. cit.* (note 47), p. 157-158, 179; A. Boutroue, *loc. cit.* (note 31), p. 28.

[260]1860s - Generals A.K. Abramov (collections made in Samarkand and in Ferghana), K.P. von Kaufmann, M.G. Chernyaev, G.A. Kolpakovsky (collections made in the Kuldja district of China); 1880s - Colonel M. Alikhanov-Avarsky; 1900-1910 - Generals A.S. Galkin, S.M. Dukhovskoy, Mishchenko. Only V.V. Vereshchagin (1860s), N.N. Karazin, A.L. Kun and N.K. Romanov (all three in the 1870s) had no military ranks, though they participated in military operations. A certain Bek in the 1900s also made a big collection of arms, which he was going to sell abroad (*Sredneaziatskaja zhizn'* [Life in Central Asia], 1907, N° 185-187).

[261]L.G. Levteeva, *Prisoedinenie Srednej Azii k Rossii v memuarnykh istochnikakh (istoriografija problemy)* [The Annexation of Central Asia to Russia as Described in the Memoir sources (Historiography of the Problem)], Tashkent, 1986, 142 p.

[262]V.s.: Chapter "Other Ways of Acquiring Objects for Collections", Paragraph "Seizure at War and Contributions".

[263]H. Moser, *op. cit.* (note 47), p. 336.

[264]A.A. Shishov, "Sarty. Etnograficheskoe i antropologicheskoe issledovanie [The Sarts. An Ethnographical and Anthropological Study]", *Sbornik materialov dlja statistiki Syr-Dar'inskoj oblasti* [Collected Statistical Materials for the Syr-Darya Region], Pt. 1, Tashkent, 1904, p.

151, 153.

[265] V.V. Krestovskij, *op. cit.* (note 38).

[266] D. Ivanov, *Soldatskoe zhit'e. Ocherki iz Turkestanskoj zhizni* [Life of a Soldier. Sketches of Turkestan Life], Saint-Petersburg, 1875, p. 204.

[267] Mak-Gakhan, *op. cit.* (note 219).

[268] Later A. Boutroue, who travelled around Turkestan in 1896, wrote that a carpet measuring 7.10 m by 3.20 m cost 1,000 roubles or 2,750 francs in Merv (A. Boutroue, *loc. cit.* (note 31), p. 18), and by the 1900s, good old Turkmenian carpets cost 75-100 roubles per square metre, and modern ones 7-10 roubles per square meter (F.A. Mikhajlov, *Tuzemcy Zakaspijskoj oblasti i ikh zhizn'. Etnograficheskij ocherk* [The native population of the Trans-Caspian Region and Their Life. An Ethnographical Survey], Ashkhabad, 1900).

[269] A.A. Olsuf'ev, V.P. Panaev, *Po Zakaspijskoj voennoj zheleznoj doroge. Putevye zametki s 43 illjustracijami* [Along the Trans-Caspian Military Railway. Travel notes with illustrations], Saint-Petersburg, 1899, p. 98.

[270] 1860s – V.V. Vereshchagin; 1870s – N.K. Romanov; 1880s – A.A. Polovtsev, I.T. Poslavsky (unpublished); 1900s – A.G. Arendorenko, A.A. Bogolyubov, N.F. Burdukov, A.A. Falkersam; 1910s – A.S. Galkin, D.K. Trepev.

[271] R. Pinner, *The Rickmers collection: Turkoman rugs in the Ethnographic Museum Berlin*, with contributions by Siawosch U. Azadi & Gisela Dombrowski, [Berlin], Museum für Völkerkunde, Staatliche Museen zu Berlin, Preussischer Kulturbesitz, 1993, 87 p.

[272] *Zakaspijskaja oblast'* [The Trans-Caspian Region], Ashkhabad, Izd. K.M. Fedorova, 1902.

[273] See note 250.

[274] Transferred to the Dashkova Ethnographic Museum, together with two Tajik costumes and other "objects from Turkestan", registered under N° 461-610 (149 in total). G.N. Chabrov, *Istorija...*, *op. cit.* (note 36), p. 20.

[275] Collection made in 1902, at the Museum of Anthropology and Ethnography (Kunstkamera, Nr. 689): S.P. Rusejkina, *loc.cit.* (note 99), p. 80.

[276]Popular musical instruments from the collections of A.N. Samoilovich (1908) are at the Museum of Anthropology and Ethnography (Kunstkamera, Nr. 1268): V.A. Prishchepova, *op.cit.* (note 71), p. 67.

[277]At the State Museum of Ethnography in Saint-Petersburg.

[278]Musical instruments from Khiva, collected in 1882, currently at the Museum of Anthropology and Ethnography (Kunstkamera): V.A. Prishchepova, *op.cit.* (note 71), p. 18.

[279]A dutar and a karnai from Darvaz, 1885; now at the Museum of Anthropology and Ethnography (Kunstkamera, Nr. 298): S.P. Rusejkina, *loc.cit.* (note 99), p. 64; V.A. Prishchepova, *op.cit.* (note 71), p. 20.

[280]Collections, since 1899, at the Museum of Anthropology and Ethnography (Kunstkamera, Nr. 474 and 478): V.A. Prishchepova, *op.cit.* (note 71), p. 36-37.

[281]Collection, since 1908, at the Museum of Anthropology and Ethnography (Kunstkamera, Nr. 1322): V.A. Prishchepova, *op.cit.* (note 71), p.51.

[282]Collections at the Museum of Ethnography in Saint-Petersburg: Nr. 1272, 1276, 1306, 1313: S.P. Rusejkina, *loc.cit.* (note 99), p. 49.

[283]A dutar, a rabob and a flute collected in the period 1876-1884 in Shugnan and Baldjuan; now in the Museum of Anthropology and Ethnography (Kunstkamera, Nr. 148, 5551): V.A. Prishchepova, *op.cit.* (note 71), p. 18; S.P. Rusejkina, *loc.cit.* (note 99), p. 64.

[284]Collected in 1915-1916 in Bukhara.

[285]Collection at the Museum of Anthropology and Ethnography (Kunstkamera, Nr. 1753): S.P. Rusejkina, *loc.cit.* (note 99), p. 80.

[286]Ch.-E. Ujfalvy, *Atlas des étoffes, op. cit.* (notes 50, 182), pl. XVI.

[287]See note 179.

[288]Esther Fihl, *Nomads of the Pamir Plateau*, New York, Thames and Hudson, 1999. About the collection made by O. Olufsen see: *Mongolian jewellery, Researches on the silver jewellery collected on the 1st and 2nd Danish Central Asian expeditions led by Henning Haslund-Christensen 1936-37 and 1938-39*, Nationalmuseets skrifter, etnografisk række, 5, København, Gyldendal, 1952; Martha Boyer, Ida Nicolaisen, *Mongolian jewellery: jewellery collected on the first and second Danish Central Asian expeditions*, New York, Thames and Hudson; Copenhagen, Rhodos

International Science and Art Publishers, 1995.

[289]Ch.-E. Ujfalvy, *Atlas des étoffes, op. cit.* (note 182), pl. XVII.

[290]L. Poliakov, *Le mythe* aryen, Paris, Calmann-Lévy, 1994; S. Gorshenina, Cl. Rapin, *Les archéologues en Asie centrale: de Kaboul à Samarcande*, Découvertes Gallimard, Paris, 2001, p. 33-35; M. Laruelle, *Le mythe aryen en Russie au XIXe siècle. La création d'une cosmologie nationale, entre science et idéologie*, Thèse de doctorat, INALCO, 2002.

[291]A. Bobrinskij, *oc. cit.* (note 232). A review by V. Stasov in: *Zapiski Vostochnogo otdelenija Russkogo arkheologicheskogo obshchestva* [Proceedings of the Oriental Department of the Russian Archaeological Society], t. 14, vyp. 1, Saint-Petersburg, 1901, p. 43-49.

[292]Collection at the Museum of Anthropology and Ethnography (Kunstkamera, Nr. 1905): V.A. Prishchepova, *op.cit.* (note 71), p. 52.

[293]Collection of manuscripts transferred to the Asiatic Museum; ethnographic collections totalling 364 objects at the Museum of Anthropology and Ethnography (Kunstkamera, Nr. 2352, 2674, 2780, 2682, 2779): V.A. Prishchepova, *op.cit.* (note 71), p. 71-72. About manuscripts see: V.A. Ivanov, "Ismailistskie rukopisi Aziatskogo muzeja (sobranie I. Zarubina 1916 g.) [Ismailian manuscripts from the Asiatic Museum]", *Izvestija Akademii nauk,* VI ser., t. XI, 1917, n° 6, p. 37-43.

[294]Collection at the Museum of Anthropology and Ethnography (Kunstkamera, Nr. 954): V.A. Prishchepova, *op.cit.* (note 71), p. 40.

[295]Collections at the Museum of Anthropology and Ethnography (Kunstkamera, Nr. 1465): S.P. Rusejkina, *loc.cit.* (note 99), p. 64.

[296]Collections of objects and photographs at the Museum of Anthropology and Ethnography (Kunstkamera, Nr. 1473, 3028, 2122, 2301, 2302): V.A. Prishchepova, *op.cit.* (note 71), p. 53. Collection 1492 of the Museum of Ethnography: S.P. Rusejkina, *loc.cit.* (note 99), p. 66.

[297]His collection is now at the Museum of Anthropology and Ethnography (Kunstkamera, Nr. 787): S.P. Rusejkina, *loc.cit.* (note 99), p. 71.

[298]Collection (8 objects) at the Museum of Anthropology and Ethnography (Kunstkamera, Nr. 5549): S.P. Rusejkina, *loc.cit.* (note 99), p. 47.

[299]Collection at the Museum of Anthropology and Ethnography (Kunstkamera, Nr. 2677): V.A. Prishchepova, *op.cit.* (note 71), p. 54-59.

[300]Collection at the Museum of Ethnography in Saint-Petersburg, Nr. 1037 and 2404: S.P. Rusejkina, *loc.cit.* (note 99), p. 81.

[301]Collection at the Museum of Ethnography in Saint-Petersburg, Nr. 1062: S.P. Rusejkina, *loc.cit.* (note 99), p. 81.

[302]Collection at the Museum of Anthropology and Ethnography (Kunstkamera, Nr. 439): V.A. Prishchepova, *op.cit.* (note 71), p. 37-38.

[303]Collection at the Museum of Ethnography in Saint-Petersburg, Nr. 1471: S.P. Rusejkina, *loc.cit.* (note 99), p. 81.

[304]Collections of traditional everyday objects and collection of photographs at the Museum of Anthropology and Ethnography (Kunstkamera, Nr. 403, 410 and 411): S.P. Rusejkina, *loc.cit.* (note 99), p. 79-80; V.A. Prishchepova, *op.cit.* (note 71), p. 35-36.

[305]Collection at the Museum of Anthropology and Ethnography (Kunstkamera, Nr. 689): S.P. Rusejkina, *loc.cit.* (note 99), p. 80.

[306]Collection at the Museum of Ethnography in Saint-Petersburg, Nr. 3378: S.P. Rusejkina, *loc.cit.* (note 99), p. 82.

[307]Collection at the Museum of Ethnography in Saint-Petersburg, Nr. 749 and 750: S.P. Rusejkina, *loc.cit.* (note 99), p. 81.

[308]Collection at the Museum of Ethnography in Saint-Petersburg, 1438-1650: S.P. Rusejkina, *loc.cit.* (note 99), p. 82.

[309]Collection at the Museum of Anthropology and Ethnography (Kunstkamera, Nr. 439): S.P. Rusejkina, *loc.cit.* (note 99), p. 80.

[310]Collection at the Museum of Anthropology and Ethnography (Kunstkamera, Nr. 1753): S.P. Rusejkina, *loc.cit.* (note 99), p. 80; V.A. Prishchepova, *op.cit.* (note 71), p. 51-52.

[311]Collections at the Museum of Anthropology and Ethnography (Kunstkamera, Nr. 2342, 2343, 2431, 2451, 2528): S.P. Rusejkina, *loc.cit.* (note 99), p. 80; V.A. Prishchepova, *op.cit.* (note 71), p. 59-60.

[312]Collections totalling more than 300 traditional objects from everyday life and a collection of photographs and drawings at the Museum of Anthropology and Ethnography (Kunstkamera, Nr. 1289, 1458, 1459, 1327, 1483, 1749, 1774, 1766): S.P. Rusejkina, *loc.cit.* (note 99), p. 80, 81; V.A. Prishchepova, *op.cit.* (note 71), p. 65.

[313]R. Karutc, *Sredi kirgizov i Turkmen na Mangyshlake* [Among the Kirghiz and Turkmen in Mangyshlak], Saint-Petersburg, 1910; R. von

Karutz, *Unter Kirgisen und Turkmenen, aus dem Leben der Steppe*, Leipzig, Klinkhardt und Biermann, 1911, VII-218 p.

[314]Collection at the Moscow Museum of the Peoples of the USSR, Nr. 5661-6026: S.P. Rusejkina, *loc.cit.* (note 99), p. 50.

[315]Collection at the Museum of Anthropology and Ethnography (Kunstkamera, Nr. 2785): S.P. Rusejkina, *loc.cit.* (note 99), p. 48.

[316]Collections at the Museum of Ethnography in Saint-Petersburg, Nr. 5119, 3234: S.P. Rusejkina, *loc.cit.* (note 99), p. 49.

[317]Collection at the Museum of Ethnography, Nr. 3522: S.P. Rusejkina, *loc.cit.* (note 99), p. 66.

[318]Collection Nr. 1 at the Moscow Museum of the Peoples of the USSR: S.P. Rusejkina, *loc.cit.* (note 99), p. 50.

[319]Collection Nr. 4 at the Moscow Museum of the Peoples of the USSR, transferred from the State Museum Fund in 1918: S.P. Rusejkina, *loc.cit.* (note 99), p. 50.

[320]Collection at the Moscow Museum of the Peoples of the USSR, Nr. 9397-9418: S.P. Rusejkina, *loc.cit.* (note 99), p. 50.

[321]Collections at the Museum of Ethnography in Saint-Petersburg, Nr. 1272, 1276, 1306, 1313; other collections comprise clothes, jewels and carpets, Nr. 836, 838 and 837: S.P. Rusejkina, *loc.cit.* (note 99), p. 49, 76.

[322]Collections of jewellery and photographs at the Museum of Anthropology and Ethnography (Kunstkamera, Nr. 1288, 1307, 1485, 1486 and 1509): V.A. Prishchepova, *op.cit.* (note 71), p. 40-50.

[323]Collections at the Museum of Anthropology and Ethnography (Kunstkamera, Nr. 340): V.A. Prishchepova, *op.cit.* (note 71), p. 18.

[324]Collection given, in 1889, to the Museum of Anthropology and Ethnography (Kunstkamera, Nr. 11): S.P. Rusejkina, *loc.cit.* note 99, p. 75.

[325]Collections at the State Museum of Ethnography, Nr. 1414, 3111: S.P. Rusejkina, *loc.cit.* (note 99), p. 76.

[326]The other Stolyariov's collections from Samarkand are at the Museum of Anthropology and Ethnography (Kunstkamera, Nr. 1253): S.P. Rusejkina, *loc.cit.* (note 99), p. 47.

[327]Collection at the Museum of Anthropology and Ethnography (Kunstkamera, Nr. 219): S.P. Rusejkina, *loc.cit.* (note 99), p. 47. This collection also comprises an important collection of clothes, which

Ukhtomsky bought in Samarkand: V.A. Prishchepova, *op.cit.* (note 71), p. 12-13, 16, 18.

[328] At present, Dudin's collections are divided up between the Museum of Anthropology and Ethnography (Kunstkamera, Nr. 778, 493) and the State Museum of Ethnography in Saint-Petersburg (collections 12-14, 16, 18-22, 24, 26, 31-34, 36-37, 39, 58-60, 238-242, 244, 245, 362, 363, 1435). See: S.P. Rusejkina, *loc. cit.* (note 99), p. 40, 47, 49, 66, 72, 75, 80, 81; V.A. Prishchepova, *op.cit.* (note 71), p. 62-65; V.A. Vishneveckaja (Prishchepova), "Iz jizni i dejatel'nosti S.M. Dudina – khudojnika, sobiratelja, issledovatelja [On S.M. Dudin's life and activities: the artist, collector, researcher]", *Iz istorii formirovanija etnograficheskikh kollekcij v muzejakh Rossii (XIX-XX vv.)* [On the history of the formation of the ethnographical collections in the Russian Museums, 19th-20th centuries], Saint-Petersburg, 1992, p. 84-106.

[329] Collections at the Museum of Anthropology and Ethnography (Kunstkamera, Nr. 1268, 1271, 1270, 1276, 3174, 1272, 1275, 1916, 3175): S.P. Rusejkina, *loc.cit.* (note 99), p. 47, 75; V.A. Prishchepova, *op.cit.* (note 71), p. 66-67.

[330] N.N. Shcherbina-Kramarenko and B.F. Romberg's collections are at the Museum of Anthropology and Ethnography (Kunstkamera, Nr. 1487 and 2265): S.P. Rusejkina, *loc.cit.* (note 99), p. 47; V.A. Prishchepova, *op.cit.* (note 71), p. 54, 67.

[331] S. Gorshenina, "Premiers pas...", *loc. cit.* (note 34).

[332] N.S. Lykoshin, "Ocherk arkheologicheskikh izyskanij v Turkestanskom krae do uchrezhdenija Turkestanskogo kruzhka ljubitelej arkheologii" [An Outline of Archaeological Research in the Turkestan Region before the Foundation of the Turkestanian Circle of Friends of Archaeology], *Protokoly Turkestanskogo kruzhka ljubitelej arkheologii* [Proceedings of the Turkestanian Circle of Friends of Archaeology], t. I. 1896, Tashkent, 1896, p. 1-58.

[333] CGA RUz, F. I-1, cat. 11, f. 240, p. 167.

[334] *Ibidem*, p. 6.

[335] N° 25, 4 July 1887.

[336] V.V. Vereshchagin, "Ot Orenburga do Tashkenta [From Orenburg to Tashkent]", *Vsemirnyj puteshestvennik* [The World Traveller], 1874, N° 5; *Materialy dlja statistiki Turkestanskogo kraja* [Statistical Materials for the

Turkestan Region]. Izd. Turkestanskogo statisticheskogo komiteta pod red. N.A. Maeva [Published by the Turkestan Statistical Committee, ed. by N.A. Maev], Vol. 3, Saint-Petersburg, 1874; G.N. Chabrov, *Vzgljady V.V. Stasova na iskusstvo narodov Srednej Azii* [V.V. Stasov's Views on the Art of Central Asian Peoples], a manuscript at CGA RUz, F. R-2681, cat. 1, f. 30, p. 4. The collection was outlined and presented in photographs: F.I. Bulgakov, *V.V. Vereshchagin i ego proizvedenija* [V.V. Vereshchagin and His Works], Saint-Petersburg, 1905.

[337] A.A. Semenov, "Nechto...", *loc. cit.* (note 44), p. 145; M.E. Masson, "Kratkij ocherk...", *loc. cit.* (note 44), p. 12.

[338] *Turkestanskie Vedomosti* [The Turkestanian News], 1880, N° 34; G.Ja. Upfal, *op. cit.* (note 112), p. 24-26.

[339] CGA RUz, F. I-5, cat. 1, f. 226, p. 8.

[340] The newspaper *Okraina* [Periphery] wrote on the 11th October, 1893: "We heard that one of the Samarkand merchants, Bukharin, had died... of cholera. According to his heirs, he left behind a valuable archaeological collection".

[341] N.I. Veselovskij, *Istorija russkogo arkheologicheskogo obshchestva za pervoe pjatidesjati-letie ego sushchestvovanija.1846-1896 gg.* [A History of the Russian Archaeological Society during the First Fifty Years of Its Existence. 1846-1896], Saint-Petersburg, 1900, p. 201.

[342] D. Evarnickij, [A description of A. Askharov's collection], *Turkestanskie Vedomosti* [The Turkestanian News], 1892, N° 31.

[343] See the full list of coins purchased by the Hermitage in: B.V. Lunin, "O numizmaticheskoj kollekcii uzbekskogo sobiratelja drevnostej Akrame Askarove", *loc. cit.* (note 224), p. 237-245.

[344] G.N. Chabrov, "Uzbeki-arkheologi...", *loc.cit.* (note 221). See also: CGA RUz, F. R-2681, cat. 345 f. 62, p 6-12.

[345] B.V. Lunin, *Srednjaja Azija v nauchnom...*, *op. cit.* (note 159), 184 p. Here one can find a description of the numismatical and archaeological collection brought from Turkestan by N.I. Veselovsky. See p. 172.

[346] *Otchet Imperatorskoj arkheologicheskoj komissii za 1882-1883 gg.* [A Report of the Imperial Archaeological Commission for 1882-1883], Saint-Petersburg, 1891, p. XI.

[347] N.I. Veselovskij, "Sushchestvujut li...", *loc. cit.* (note 61), p. 112.

[348]N.I. Veselovskij, "Persten'-pechat' Miran-shakha mirzy, syna Tamerlana [A Seal-Ring belonging to Miran-shah Mîrzâ, Son of Tamerlan]", *Kaufmanskij sbornik* [Collected Papers Dedicated to Kaufmann], Moscow, 1910, p. 229-234.

[349]Among the 1,202 objects there were Graeco-Bactrian and Indo-Greek coins (Euthydemus, Heliocles, Diodotus, Seleucus, Agathocles), Sasanid (Shapur II), Syrian (of Antioch) and Abbasid coins, coins of the Samanids, Ghazneids, Ileks, Khwaresmshahs, Timurids, Sheibanids and others: 11 gold, 77 silver and 951 copper coins. Besides, N.I. Veselovsky bought 13 copper earrings, 3 figurines (of copper, stone and clay), 18 seals, 6 stones with carved figures of men and animals and other antiques. All the things bought in 1883, as well as the objects bought later from Mîrzâ Bukhari (terracotta, fragments of ossuaries, ceramics dating from various periods, small bronze objects) were donated, in 1883-1891, to the Hermitage. Cited from B.V. Lunin, "Samarkandskij ljubitel' [...] Mirza Bukhari", *loc. cit.* (note 120), p. 35. A full catalogue of the antique collection, bought by N.I. Veselovsky from M. Bukhari, is in the archives of the Saint-Petersburg Department of the Institute of Archaeology of the Russian Academy of Sciences, F. 1, cat. 1, f. 20, 1883, p. 76-81.

[350]"Spisok predmetov kollekcij Junusova, Zargera i Bukharina [A List of Objects in the Collections of Junusov, Zarger, and Bukharin]", the archives of the Saint-Petersburg Department of the Institute of Archaeology of the Russian Academy of Sciences, F. 18, f. 462, p. 1-4.

[351]The gifts were received from A. Askarov, A.I. Vil'kens, N.V. Charykov, P.I. Khomutov, Korolkov, Voitsekhovich, Ivanov and G.A. Arendorenko. B.V. Lunin, *Srednjaja Azija v nauchnom...*, *op. cit.* (note 159), p. 173.

[352]G.Ja. Upfal, *Istorija Samarkandskogo muzeja* [A History of Samarkand Museum], manuscript in N. Almazova's private archives (Samarkand), p. 29.

[353] B.V. Lunin, "Orientalist-Turkestanoved Evgenij Fedorovich Kal' [Orientalist and Expert in Turkestan Evgeni Fedorovich Kal']", *Trudy Tashkentskogo Gosudarstvennogo Universiteta. Arkheologija Srednej Azii* [Transactions of the Tashkent State University. Archaeology of Central Asia], Vol. VII, Tashkent, 1966, p. 106-124.

[354]*Turkestanskie Vedomosti* [The Turkestanian News], 1891, N° 39; G.N. Chabrov, *Istorija...*, *op.cit.* (note 36), p. 39; N.S. Sadykova, *op. cit.*

(note 113), p. 41.

[355] E. Kal', *Persidskie, arabskie i tjurkskie rukopisi Turkestanskoj publichnoj biblioteki* [Persian, Arabian and Turkic Manuscripts of the Turkestan Public Library], Tashkent, Tipografija okruzhnogo shtaba, 1899, 77 p.

[356] Anonymous article in: *Okraina* [Periphery], 1892, N° 1147.

[357] V. Tizengauzen, "Novoe sobranie vostochnykh monet A.V. Komarova [A New Collection of Oriental Coins]", *Zapiski Imperatorskogo arkheologicheskogo obshchestva* [Transactions of the Imperial Archaeological Society], Vol. 3, Saint-Petersburg, 1888, p. 51-84; E. Ukhtomskij, *Ot Kalmyckoj stepi do Bukhary* [From the Kalmyk Steppe to Bukhara], Saint-Peresburg, 1891, p. 7, 101. According to M.E. Masson, his collection is deposited in the Historical Museum in Moscow (note 62); but, according to B.V. Lunin, 3000 coins of his last collection are at the Hermitage (B.V. Lunin, *op. cit.*, 1980, p. 88, 93). According to A. Banck (ref. *Addenda, infra*, p. 205), p. 7, the numismatic collection of Komarov was at the Hermitage from 1892.

[358] Now in the State Museum of Ethnography in Saint-Petersburg.

[359] S. Gorshenina, "V.V. Krestovskij: "Antigeroj" sredneaziatskoj arkheologii ? [V.V. Krestovsky, an "Anti-Hero" of Central Asian Archaeology ?]", *Materialy konferencii IIMK "Kul'turnoe nasledie Vostoka"* [Proceedings of the Conference "Cultural Heritage of the Orient"], Saint-Petersburg, 1999, p. 22-26.

[360] D.I. Evarnickij, *Putevoditel' po Srednej Azii ot Baku do Tashkenta v arkheologicheskom i istoricheskom otnoshenijakh* [An Archaeological and Historical Guide to Central Asia from Baku to Tashkent], Tashkent, 1893, p. 110.

[361] CGA RUz, F. I-1, cat. 15, f. 460, p. 2.

[362] V.A. Shishkin, *loc. cit.* (note 63), p. 22.

[363] S.F. Ol'denburg, "Pamjati Nikolaja Fedorovicha Petrovskogo (1837-1908) [In Memory of Nikolai Fedorovich Petrovsky]", *Zapiski Vostochnogo otdelenija russkogo arkheologicheskogo obshchestva* [Proceedings of the Oriental Department of the Russian Archaeological Society], t. 20, Saint-Petersburg, 1912, p. 1-8; A.A. Semenov, "Nechto...", *loc. cit.* (note 44), p. 145; G. Kizerickij, "Khotanskie drevnosti iz sobranija N.F. Petrovskogo [Khotan Antiques from the Collection of N.F.

Petrovsky]", *Zapiski Vostochnogo Otdelenija Russkogo Arkheologicheskogo Obshchestva* [Proceedings of the Oriental Department of the Russian Archaeological Society], Vol. 9, 1896, p. 167-190; N.V. D'jakonova, S.S. Sorokin, *Khotanskie drevnosti. Katalogue Khotanskikh drevnostej, khranjashchikhsja v Otdele Vostoka Gosudarstvennogo Ermitazha. Terrakota i shtuk* [Khotan Antiques. A Catalogue of Khotan Antiques in the Oriental Department of the Hermitage. Terracotta and Stucco], Leningrad, 1960; G.N. Chabrov, *Nikolaj Fedorovich Petrovskij i sud'ba ego biblioteki i kollekcii* [Nikolaj Fedorovitch Petrovsky and his library and collection sort], Communication at the 53rd meeting of the Scientific Circle for Central Asian Studies, June 14th, 1962, manuscript, CGA RUz, F. R-2681, cat. 1, f. 321, p. 1; *Turkestanskie vedomosti* [The Turkestanian News], 1897, N 22.

364 G.Ja. Upfal, *op. cit.* (note 112), p. 65.

365 CGA RUz, F. R-2681, cat. 1, f. 1065, p 1.

366 G.N. Chabrov, *Chastnoe kollekcionerstvo...*, *op. cit.* (note 159), p. 14.

367 B.V. Lunin, *Istoriografija...*, *op. cit.* (note 159), p. 295-298.

368 S. Gorshenina, "Kollekcija antikov I.T.Poslavskogo: sozdanie, razvitie, ischeznovenie" [I.T. Poslavsky's Collection of Antiques: Its Making, Development and Disappearance], *Iskusstvo Uzbekistana: drevnost', srednevekov'e, sovremennost'* [Arts in Uzbekistan: Antiquity, the Middle Ages and the Modern Time], Tashkent, I, 1995, p. 17-18.

369 M.E. Masson, "Gorodishcha Starogo Termeza i ikh izuchenie [Archaeological Sites of Old Termez and the Research in Them]", *Trudy Uzbekistanskogo filiala Akademii nauk SSSR*, ser. 1, Istorija, Arkheologija [Transactions of Uzbekistan Department of the Academy of Sciences of the USSR. Series 1: History and Archaeology], Vol. 2, Tashkent, 1940, p. 21, 25.

370 A.A. Semenov, "Nechto...", *loc. cit.* (note 44), p. 145; G.A. Pugachenkova, "Tri akhemenidskie gemmy iz sobranija muzeja istorii UzSSR [Three Akhemenid Gems in the Collection of the Museum of History of the Uzbek Soviet Socialist Republic]", *Trudy muzeja istorii UzSSR* [Transactions of the Museum of History of the Uzbek SSR], Vol. 3, Tashkent, 1956, p. 81-87; N.E. Vundcettel', "Interesnaja gemma iz kollekcii Turkestanskogo Vostochnogo Instituta [A Curious Gem in the

Collection of the Turkestan Oriental Institute]", *Sbornik Turkestanskogo Vostochnogo Instituta v chest' professora A.E. Shmita* [Collected Papers Dedicated to Prof. A.E. Schmit, ed. by the Turkestan Oriental Institute], Tashkent, 1923, p. 146.

[371] M.E. Masson, *Tri epizoda, svjazannye s Samarkandskimi pamjatnikami stariny* [Three Episodes Connected with Samarkand Ancient Monuments], Tashkent, 1972, p. 8.

[372] CGA RUz, F. I-71, cat. 1, f. 22a, p. 64.

[373] Cited from B.V. Lunin, *Iz istorii russkogo vostokovedenija i arkheologii v Turkestane (Turkestanskij kruzhok ljubitelej arkheologii (1895-1917)* [From the History of Russian Oriental Studies in Turkestan (The Turkestanian Circle of Friends of Archaeology)], Tashkent, 1958, p. 77.

[374] N.E. Vundcettel', *loc. cit.* (note 370), p. 146.

[375] B.V. Lunin, *Vostochnyj fakul'tet (Kratkij ocherk istorii vostfaka TashGU)* [The Oriental Faculty (An Outline of the History of the Oriental Faculty of the Tashkent State University)], Tashkent, 1981, p. 16.

[376] V.S. Minosjanc, *loc.cit.* (note 237), p. 7.

[377] O. Ju. Poslavskaja, "Moj Tashkent. Dvadcatye gody [My Tashkent. 1920s]", *Zvezda Vostoka* [The Star of the Orient], 1989, N° 11, p. 150.

[378] S. Gorshenina, "Turkestanskaja kollekcija Leona Barshchevskogo i ee sledy v Uzbekistane, Francii, Pol'she i Rossii" [The Turkestan Collection of Leon Barszcewski and Traces of it in Uzbekistan, France, Poland and Russia], *Obshchestvennoe mnenie. Uzbekistanskij gumanitarnyj zhurnal* [Public Opinion. The Uzbekistan Journal of Humanities], Tashkent, 1998, N° 2, p. 144-149. Barszscewski's collection of photographs is in the Muzeum Historii Fotografii w Krakowie. An exhibition of biographical documents "Leon Barszscewski. Zapomniany badacz Azji Srodkowej" [Leon Barszscewski. A Forgotten Explorer of Central Asia] was prepared in 1995 by Marzene Godzinska at the Muzeum Azji i Pacyfiku, Warsaw (and held in 1996). See catalogue of the exhibition: *"Leon Barszczewski - Zapomniany Badacz Azji Srodkowej (1876-1896)"*. Barszscewski's collection and his portrait are shown in photographs taken by I. Strojetsky, in the article: M.M. Blombergova, "Badania archeologiczne Polakòw na terytorium Imperium Rosyjskiego w XIX i poczatku XX wieku", *Acta archaeologica Lodziensia*, N° 37, Lodz, 1993, p. 106-107.

[379] D.I. Evarnickij, "K voprosu...", *op.cit.* (note 111).

[380]CGA RUz, F. I-1, cat. 11, f. 1060, p. 1-18. He also possessed an important mineralogical collection.

[381]N.I. Reshetnikov's collection consisted of about 1,000 objects, including: terracottas (434), pendants (5), a seal, clay toys (17), ceramics (the earliest specimens date back to the 14th century (31), lamps from the 14th and 15th centuries (3), an implement for smoking meat, jars (12), fragments of ossuaries (56) and fragments of architectural monuments (30). Among the coins, there were 67 golden, 316 silver ones and "an unsorted heap". The collection included ethnological materials as well. About the donation of the collection see: *Spravochnaja knizhka Samarkandskoj oblasti na 1897* god [A Handbook of the Samarkand Region for 1897], Vol. 5, Samarkand, 1897 (Letopis' Samarkandskoj oblasti, sostavlennaja po rukopisi grafa Nikolaja Jakovlevicha Rostovskogo M. Virskim, 9 janvarja 1896 g., [Chronograph of the Samarkand Region. 9th January, 1896]), p. 252.

[382]CGA RUz, F. R-2681, cat. 1, f. 1065, p. 1.

[383]"Popolnenie muzeja [The Growth of the Museum Funds)]", *Turkestanskie Vedomosti* [The Turkestanian News], 1896, August 1 (13), N° 57.

[384]J. Chaffanjon's Diary, Book 1, p. 30. The Chaffanjon Family Archives (Paris).

[385]V.V. Bartol'd, "Otchet o komandirovke v Turkestan [A Report on the Trip to Turkestan] "*Zapiski Vostochnogo Otdelenija russkogo arkheologicheskogo obshchestva* [Proceedings of the Oriental department of the Russian Archaeological Society], t. 15, vyp. 2-3, Saint-Petersburg, 1904, p. 219; I.A. Sukharev, "Kollekcija V.L. Vjatkina [V.L. Vyatkin's Collection]", *Problemy istorii dokapitalisticheskikh obshchestv* [Problems of the History of Pre-Capitalist Societies], Moscow, 1934, N° 7-8, p. 173; V.A. Prishchepova, *op.cit.* (note 71), p. 53. Photographs of the Vyatkin archaeological collection are at the Museum of History and Culture of the Peoples of Uzbekistan (Reghistan, Samarkand).

[386]M.E. Masson, "Kratkij ocherk...", *loc. cit.* (note 44), p. 12.

[387]*Protokoly Turkestanskogo kruzhka ljubitelej Arkheologii* [Proceedings of the Turkestanian Circle of Friends of Archaeology], god XII, Tashkent, 1908.

[388]M.E. Masson, "Gorodishcha...", *loc. cit.* (note 369).

[389]M.V. Stolyarov's collection of ceramics is shown in a photograph, taken in 1914, in the article: Ch.K. Wilkinson, "The Glazed Pottery of Nishapur and Samarkand", *Bulletin of the Metropolitan Museum of Art*, 1961, November, p. 102-110. Part of his collection of ceramics was bought in 1908 by the Museum of Anthropology and Ethnography (Kunstkamera, Nr. 1248,1253): V.A. Prishchepova, *op. cit.* (note 71), p. 69.

[390]C. Gorshenina, "Central'naja Azija v tvorchestve Zhozefa-Antuana Kastan'e [Central Asia in the Works of J.-A. Castagné]", *Vostok-Oriens: istorija i sovremennost' afro-aziatskikh obshchestv* [The East – Oriens. The Past and the Present of Afro-Asian Societies], Moscow, 1999, N° 1, p. 130-147. See also a review by B.V. Litvinsky: "Joseph-Antoine Castagné: Researcher and Scholar or Amateur Student of Local Lore ?", *ibidem*, p. 147-155; S. Gorshenina, "Un précurseur de l'archéologie et de l'ethnologie françaises en Asie centrale: Joseph-Antoine Castagné (1875-1958)", *Comptes rendus de l'Académie des Inscriptions et Belles-Lettres* (Paris), séance du 7 mars 1997, p. 255-272.

[391]V.V. Bartol'd, "Otchet o komandirovki v Turkestanskij Kraj letom 1916 g.", *Sobranie sochinenij* [Collected Works], t. VIII, 1973, p. 337.

[392]"Spisok predmetov, postupivshikh v muzej Orenburgskoj Uchenoj Arkhivnoj komissii za 1916 god [A List of Objects Received by the Museum of Orenburg's Learned Archives Committee in 1916]", *Trudy Orenburgskoj Ucenoj Arkhivnoj komissii* [Proceedings of the Orenburg Learned Archives Committee], Vol. XXXV, Orenburg, 1917.

[393]*Izvestija Turkestanskogo otdela Imperatorskogo russkogo geografícheskogo obshchestva* [Proceedings of the Turkestan Department of the Imperial Russian Geographical Society], Vol. X, Pt. 2, ch. 1, T., 1915, p. 51; CGA RUz, F. I-69, Cat. 1, f. 61, p. 73, 78.

[394]M.E. Masson, *Padajushchij minaret* [The Falling Minaret], Tashkent, 1968, p. 24-25; V.S. Minosjanc, *loc.cit.* (note 237), p. 22-23; CGA RUz, F. I-72, cat. 1, f. 14, p. 18; *Ibidem*, F. R-396, cat. 1, f. 54. Some of Castagné's works (manuscripts, photographs and drawings) were given by his daughter, Olga Iosifovna Tikhonovich, to L. Miroshnikov in 1967. Unfortunately, I did not gain admission to these archives, although - while working on the article about Castagné - I contacted L. Miroshnikov personally. The latter, in turn, did not take into consideration recent data on Castagné in his article. See: L. Miroshnikov, "The Moslem mazars of western China" by Nikolay Pantusov and the archives of Joseph Castagné",

Information bulletin of the International association for the study of the cultures of Central Asia, issue 22, Moscow, 2000, p. 20-48.

[395] 1850s – 100%; 1860s – 20%; 1870s – 39%; 1880s – 53%; 1890s – 33%; 1900s – 22%; 1910s – 20%. A. Naymark mentions a Shumilov's publication (1910), where the author pointed out and listed 45 coins collectors in Central Asia (*loc. cit.* [note 18], n. 48).

[396] G.N. Chabrov, *Istorija..., op.cit.* (note 36), p. 20. The widow donated the collection to the Hermitage in 1904: A. Banck, *infra*, p. 205.

[397] P.I. Lerkh, "Monety Bukhar-Khudatov [The Coins of Bukharan Khudats]", *Trudy Vostochnogo otdelnija Imperatorskogo Russkogo Arkheologicheskogo obshchestv* [Transactions of the Oriental Department of the Imperial Russian Archaeological Soc.], 18, Saint-Petersburg, 1909.

[398] *Katalog Turkestanskogo otdela Vserossijskoj Politekhnicheskoj vystavki 1872 g.* [Catalogue of the Turkestan Department of the All-Russian Polytechnic Exhibition of 1872], Moscow, 1872, p. 3, 53, 73.

[399] 13% of the overall number of Russian collections.

[400] N.I. Veselovskij, "Pamjatnik Khodzha Akhrara v Samarkande [The Monument of Khodja Akhrar in Samarkand]", *Vostochnye Zapiski* [Oriental Papers], Saint-Petersburg, 1895; S.M. Dudin, "Ornamentika i sovremennoe sostojanie starinnykh Samarkandskikh mechetej [Ornaments and the Present State of Old Samarkand Mosques]", *Izvestija Russkoj arkheologicheskoj Komissii* [Proceedings of the Russian Archaeological Committee], Vol. 7, Saint-Petersburg, 1903; Shubinskij, *op.cit.*(note 45); V.D. Sokolov, *Moskva-Samarkand (Putevye vpechatlenija)* [Moscow – Samarkand. Travel Impressions], Moscow, 1894. See also note 122.

[401] Today the panel is at the Hermitage (AFR 4992). See: *Asie des steppes d'Alexandre le Grand a Gengis Khan,* Catalogue de l'exposition a Musee Guimet, Paris, 2000, p. 106.

[402] Quoted from M. Durdyev, *loc. cit.* (note 54).

[403] V. Dukhovskaya, *op.cit.* (note 69).

[404] CGA RUz, F. R-1591, cat. 1, f. 7, p. 1.

[405] Quoted from G.N. Chabrov, *Istorija..., op.cit.* (note 36), p. 69.

[406] CGA RUz, F. I-1, cat. 20, f. 4148, p. 11, 11 verso.

[407] A. Desreumaux, "Stèles syriaques nestoriennes", *Recueil des inscriptions lapidaires ouest-sémitiques du Musée des Beaux-Arts et du*

Muséum d'Histoire naturelle de Lyon, 2000, n° 2-3, p. 60.

[408] For a detailed history of collecting and studying manuscripts see: B.V. Lunin, *Srednjaja Azija v dorevoljucionnom...*, *op. cit.* (note 84); A.I. Kormilicyn, *Rukopisnye kollekcii i biblioteki na territorii Uzbekistana epokhi srednevekov'ja* [Manuscript Collections and Libraries on the Territory of Mediaeval Uzbekistan], Tashkent, Institut rukopisej AN RUz i Tashkentskij gosudarstvennyj institut kul'tury [The Institute of Manuscripts of the AS of the Uzbek Rebublic and Tashkent State Institute of Culture], 1993. See also M.E. Trifonenko, *Vostochnye rukopisu i staropechatnye materialy v sobranii Rossijskoj gosudarstvennoj biblioteki (istorija formirovanija, sostav kollekcij i metodicheskie aspekty opisanija)* [Eastern manuscripts and ancient printings in the collection of the Russian State Library], Avtoreferat kandidatskoj dissertacii, Moscow, 2003.

[409] See: V.V. Krestovskij, *op.cit.* (note 38); A.N. Somojlovich, "Kratkij otchet o poezdke v Tashkent, Bukharu i v Khivinskoe khanstvo v 1908 godu [A Brief Report on the Trip to Tashkent, Bukhara and the Khivan Khanate in 1908]", *Izvestija Russkogo komiteta dlja izuchenija Srednej i Vostochnoj Azii v istoricheskom, arkheologicheskom, lingvisticheskom i etnograficheskom otnoshenijakh* [Proceedings of the Russian Committee for the study of Central and Eastern Asia with regard to Historical, Linguistic and Ethnographical Aspects], Saint-Petersburg, 1909, N° 9, p. 21-22; A.A. Semenov, "Licyvye rukopisi Bukharskoj Central'noj biblioteki [Illustrated Manuscripts of the Central Library of Bukhara]", *Iran* [Iran], p. 88-89.

[410] A.Z. Validov, "Vostochnye rukopisi v Ferganskoj oblasti [Oriental Manuscripts in the Ferghana Region]", *Zapiski Vostochnnogo Otdelenija Imperatorskogo russskogo arkheologichoskogo obshchestva* [Transactions of the Oriental Department of the Imperial Russian Archaeological Society], 22 (1913-1914), 1915, p. 303-320; *Izvestija Imperatorskoj arkheologicheskoj komissii* [Proceedings of the Imperial Archaeological Committee], Vol. 5, Saint-Petersburg, 1903; V.V. Bartol'd, "Otchet...", *loc. cit.* (note 385), p. 219; 'Abd al-Ra'ûf Fitrat, "Bayânâti sayyohi hindij", *Narq yulduzi*, n° 8, 1991, p. 3-56.

[411] Important collections in Tashkent were owned by Sharif-Khodja (a catalogue from 1912, made at the request of the Tashkent Department of the Society for Oriental Studies by Mahsud-ata Khodja Atayev, was given for the purpose of a study to the society members, N.P. Ostroumov and P.P.

Tsvetkov: *Izvestija Tashkentskogo obshchestva vostokovedenija* [Transactions of the Tashkent Society for Oriental Studies], Tashkent, 1902); Major Djurabek (23 manuscripts from his collection were given to the Oriental Institute, later the Tashkent State University. V.V. Bartol'd, "Sobranie rukopisej Dzhurabeka [Djurabek's Manuscript Collection]", *Sobranie sochinenij* [Collected Works], t. 8, Moscow, 1973, p. 313-314; *Sredneaziatskij al'manakh* [Central Asian Almanac of 1896], nauchno-literaturnyj sbornik s kalendarem na 1896 god, pod. red. E.T. Smirnova, 1985); Khairuddin-bek (A.Z. Validov, *loc.cit.*(407); *Idem*, "O sobranijakh rukopisej v Bukharskom khanstve (otchet o komandirovke)" [Collections of Manuscripts in the Bukharan Khanate], *Ibidem*, 23 (1915), 1916, p. 245-262); by the Head Kazi of Tashkent Muhitdin-Khodji (theological, historical and geographical works in Arabian, Persian and the Turkic languages); A. Askarov (of special interest are "The Collected Verses of Mirza Bidyl", "Stories from the Lives of Saints by Siyari-Sharif", "Tafsir Mishkatu Sharif").

[412]The collections of Rakhmanov (143 volumes), Fitrat (150 volumes) and Khadi Zarifov (40 volumes), of the last qazi-kalan of Bukhara Mîrzâ Muhamad Sharif Sadr-i Ziyâ, Mullâ Mukammad, Allâh-Nazar Tuqsabâ, Ghâzî Bek Tuqsabâ, Mîr Muhammad Amîn Makhdûm, Sayyid Mahmûd Tarakachî, Tûra Khwâja Sudûr, Yahyâ Khwâja Sudûr Jûybârî et Khwâja-Qul Dâdkhwân, Qazi Burhan al-Din, Hishmat Mîrzâ Siddiq-Jân, son of Emir Muzaffar.

[413]The Collections of Yunus-Djan Dadkh Muhammedov (manuscripts on the history of Kokand), and an interpreter from Ferghana, Ju.K. Kazbekov.

[414]Collections of Mîrzâ Bukhari and Sh.A. Lapin.

[415]Collections of Mullâ Muhammad Rajab, Mullâ Abû Nazar, Kamâl Biy Bazzâz, Nasral-lâh Khân Jura, Abrâr Khwâja Khatîb, Mîrzâ 'Abd Al-Qayyûm, Mîrzâ Yûnus, 'Abd Al-Qâdir Khwâja et Ghulâm Qâdir Khân.

[416]Collections of Mullâ Najm Al-dîn et Mullâ Karîm Biy (Shadman Vahidov and Aftandil Erkinov, *loc. cit.* [note 186]), and Khwâja Mohammad Pârsâ (L. Dodkhudaeva, "La bibliothèque de Khwâja Mohammad Pârsâ", *Les Cahiers d'Asie centrale*, 1998, 5-6, p. 125-146).

[417]A.A. Semenov, *Khudozhestvennaja rukopis' na territorii sovremennogo Uzbekistana* [Illuminated Manuscripts on the Territory of today's Uzbekistan], Tashkent, 1948, a manuscript preserved at the Institute of Art

named after Khamza, Tashkent.

[418] A.I. Dobrosmyslov, *Tashkent v proshlom i nastojashchem. Istoricheskij ocherk* [Tashkent in the Past and Present. A Historical Survey], Tashkent, Elektro-parovaja tipografija O.A. Parceva, 1912.

[419] From 1870, when it was opened, the Library in Tashkent systematically collected manuscripts: in 1889 its stock included 68 volumes with 126 titles. Later in 1908 the naturalist and traveller, D.N. Logofet, tried to create a special budget for the acquisition of " interesting private libraries", such as the Petrovsky's (the Russian Consul of Kashgar) library: "Chastnye knijnye sobranija i kazennaja biblioteka [Private book collection and state-controlled library]", *Turkestanskie Vedomosti* [The Turkestanian News], 1908, n° 261. In Soviet times this process continued (it is not possible to discuss the methods of collecting here). Thus, V.L. Vyatkin's collection (273 manuscripts) was bought in 1933 by the Tashkent Public Library together with the collections of Rakhmanov (143 volumes), Fitrat (150) and Khadi Zarifov (40). In 1936 the collection of the last qazi-kalan of Bukhara, Mîrzâ Muhamad Sharif Sadr-i Ziyâ (1867-1932) (300 volumes) was transferred to this library. A. Muminov, *loc. cit.* (note 96), p. 18.

[420] A.A. Semenov, "Sredneaziatskie rukopisnye fondy i vazhnost' ikh izuchenija [Central Asian Manuscript Funds and the Importance of Studying Them]", *Materialy Pervoj vsesojuznoj nauchnoj konferencii vostokovedov v Tashkente* [Proceedings of the 1st All-Union Scientific Conference of Orientalists in Tashkent], 1958, p. 914.

[421] For a bibliography on manuscript collections see: A. Muminov, *loc. cit.* (note 96), p. 24-26, 31, 33; B. Kazakov, *Bukharan Documents. The collection in the District Library, Bukhara*, translated from Russian by J. Paul, Berlin (Das Arabische Buch), 2001, 103 p.

[422] *Imperatorskaja publichnaja biblioteka za 100 let. 1814-1914* [A Hundred Years of the Imperial Public Library, 1814-1914], Saint-Petersburg, 1914; V.S. Ikonnikov, *op. cit.* (note 88). See also [V.V. Stasov], S*lavjanskij i vostochnyj ornament po rukopisjam drevnego i novogo vremeni, sobral i issledoval Vladimir Stasov* [Slav and Oriental ornament in ancient and modern manuscripts, collected and studied by V. Stasov], Saint-Petersburg, izd. A.A. Il'ina, 1887.

[423] *Aziatskij muzej – Leningradskoe otdelenie Instituta Vostokovedenija AN SSSR* [The Asiatic Museum, the Leningrad Department of the Institute

for Oriental Studies of the Academy of Sciences of the USSR], Moscow, Nauka, 1972, 595 p.

[424]P.I. Lerkh, "Monety Bukhar-khudatov", *loc. cit.* note 397, p. 52-53.

[425]A.L. Kun, "Predanie o biblioteke Tamerlana [A Legend of Tamerlan's Library]", *Materialy dlja statistiki Turkestanskogo kraja* [Statistical Materials on the Turkestan Province], Vol. 3, Saint-Petersburg, 1874; "Drevnie rukopisi v Samarkande. Biblioteka Tamerlana [Old manuscripts in Samarkand. Tamerlan's Library]", *Turkestanskie Vedomosti* [The Turkestanian News], 1970, N° 3; "Armjanskie pridanija o biblioteke Tamerlana [Armenian Legend about Tamerlan's Library]", *ibidem,* 1873, N° 44; D.N. Logofet, "Tamerlanovskaja biblioteka [Tamerlan Library]", *ibidem,* 1911, N° 24.

[426]A.F. Shebunin, "Kuficheskij koran Imperatorskoj sankt-peter-burgskoj publichnoj biblioteki [A Kufic Koran of the Imperial Saint-Petersburg Public Library]", *Zapiski Vostochnogo otdela imperatorskogo Arkheologicheskogo obshestva* [Proceedings of the Oriental Department of the Imperial Archaeological Society], 6, Saint-Petersburg, 1891, p. 69-133; A.A. Khasanov, "K istorii svjashchennogo Korana Osmana v Tashkente [Notes on the History of the Sacred Koran of Osman in Tashkent]", *Bjulleten' Gosudarstvennogo Komiteta po nauke i tekhnike Respubliki Uzbekistan* [Bulletin of the State Committee for Science and Technology of the Uzbekistan Republic], N° 1, 1997, p. 25-31.

[427]About the trips to Turkestan made by V.V. Bartold in 1893-1894, 1902, 1904 and 1916, which enabled him to make various collections, including collections of manuscripts, see: N. Akramov, "O nekotorykh materialakh po biografii V.V. Bartol'da [On Some Materials for the Biography of V.V. Bartold]", *Izvestija Otdelenija Obshchestvennykh nauk AN Tadzhikskoj SSR* [Proceedings of the Department of Social Sciences of the Academy of Sciences of the Tajik SSR], Vol. 1 (28), Dushanbe, 1962, p. 11-12. A catalogue of the manuscript collection was prepared by K.G. Saleman in 1906.

[428][A.A. Molchanov], "Perechen' rukopisej V.L. Vjatkina v Gosudarstvennoj publichnoj biblioteke UzSSR [A List of V.L. Vyatkin's Manuscripts in the State Library of the Uzbek Soviet Socialist Republic]", *Trudy gosudarstvennoj publichnoj biblioteki UzSSR* [Transactions of the State Public Library of the Uzbek SSR], t. 1, Tashkent, 1935, p. 60-91.

[429]He donated part of his collection to the Turkestan Public Library,

and in 1897 to the Asiatic Museum.

[430] In 1915, commissioned by the Asiatic Museum, he bought 1057 manuscripts in Arabian, Persian and Turkish from bookmarkets and the libraries of medressahs in Bukhara; in 1916 he bought 68 more manuscripts.

[431] He donated five manuscripts, which he had collected in Bukhara and Tashkent, to the Oriental Department of the Russian Imperial Archaeological Society.

[432] In 1871 he sent two cases of books from Shahr-i Sabz to the Saint-Petersburg Public Library; his own collection of manuscripts, bought by E.K. Gartie, was later donated to Saint-Petersburg University and to the Asiatic Museum.

[433] 32 manuscripts, bought by P.I. Lerch on his trip in 1858-1959 at the occasion of the diplomatic mission of Colonel N. Ignatyev in Bukhara and Khiva, were included in the collection of the Asiatic Museum and described by K.G. Saleman.

[434] In 1897 he sold 20 manuscripts to the Asiatic Museum, which were later described by K.G. Saleman.

[435] In 1907 he donated some manuscripts - *Risolia* - to the Turkestanian Circle of Friends of Archaeology (*Turkestanskie Vedomosti* [The Turkestanian News], 1907, n° 66, 69). After his death part of his rich library was bought by the national library Navoi in Tashkent: E.K. Betger, "Tri veka kul'turnoj raboty. K 75-ti letiju Gosudarstvennoj Publichnoj Biblioteki im. Navoi [Three centuries of cultural works. On the 75th anniversary of the State Public Library Navoi]", manuscript, CGA RUz, F. R-2681, cat. 1, f. 321, p. 1.

[436] His collection consisted of 34 manuscripts, which were later donated to the Asiatic Museum: "Materialy po sredneaziatsko-tureckoj litera-ture. 1. Kratkaja opis' sredneaziatskikh rukopisej sobranija A. Samojlovicha [Materials on Central Asian Turkish Literature. 1. A Short List of the Central Asian Manuscripts in A. Samoilovich's Collection]", *Zapiski Vostochnogo Otdelenija Rossijskogo Imperatorskogo Arkheologicheskogo obshchestva* [Proceedings of the Oriental Department of the Russian Imperial Archaeological Society], t. 19, Saint-Petersburg, 1910, p. 1-30.

[437] A.A. Semenov's manuscript collection (141 items: historical

manuscripts, Arabian-Persian poetry, treatises on Islamism, some richly decorated manuscripts from the workshops of the Timurid dynasty of the 15th century or the Khivan Khans of the 19th century), made from 1913 to 1953 and preserved today in the institute of History, Archaeology and Ethnography of the Academy of Sciences of Tadjikistan, was described by L. and L. Dodkhudoeva and O. Akimushkin in an annotated catalogue, including the scholar's notes, which unfortunately has remained unpublished up until now. About Semenov's collection see: V.V. Bartol'd, "Otchet...", *loc. cit.* (note 385); L. et L. Dodkhudoeva, "Manuscrits orientaux du Tadjikistan (la collection A.A.Semenov)", *Cahiers d'Asie centrale,* n° 7, 1999, p. 39-55.

438 B.V. Lunin, *Srednjaja Azija v dorevoljucionnom...*, *op. cit.* note 84.

439 *Adler Special Manuscript Collection, op. cit.* (note 252).

440F. Richard, *loc. cit.* (note 138), p. 61-63.

441 B.V. Lunin, *Iz istorii russkogo vostokovedenija...*, *op.cit.* (note 373), p. 40; L.I. Rempel', *op. cit.* (note 218); G.N. Chabrov "Sobiranie ornamental'nykh motivov sredneaziatskogo iskusstva v dorevoljucionnom Turkestane [The collecting of Ornament Patterns of Central Asia in Pre-Revolutionary Turkestan]", *Trudy Tashkentskogo Gosudarstvennogo Universiteta* [Proceedings of the Tashkent State University], Tashkent, 1963, Vol. 200. See also CGA RUz, F. R-2681, cat. 1, f. 90, p. 7-11.

442CGA RUz, F. R-2296, cat. 1, f. 35, p. 73; B.V. Lunin, *Istoriografija...*, *op. cit.* (note 159), p. 90.

443V.V. Krestovskij, *op.cit* (note 38), p. 72.

444N.E. Simakov, *Iskusstvo Srednej Azii. Sbornik ornamentov i uzorov, snjatykh s natury na pamjatnikakh arkhitektury i predmetakh goncharnykh, tkackikh, juvelirnykh i prochikh* [The Art of Central Asia. A Collection of Ornaments Reproduced from Architectural Monuments, Ceramics, Fabric, Carpets, Jewellery etc.], Saint-Petersburg, 1883, 50 lithographs. See. V.V. Stasov's resumé in: *Russkij biograficheskij slovar'* [Russian biographical dictionary]. Tom Sabaneev-Smyslov, Saint-Petersburg, 1904, p. 447.

445The collection of water-colours with Kazakh ornaments collected in the Semipalatinsk Region in 1913 is at the Museum of Anthropology and Ethnography (Kunstkamera, n° 2519). V.A. Prishchepova, *op.cit.* (note 71), p. 76.

446His album containing 9 water-colours is in Uzbekistan at the

National Library Navoi.

[447] A. Astaf'ev, *Tekinskie ornamenty s ikh primeneniem dlja kovrov, vyshivok i prochego, sobrannye A. Astaf'evym v Akhal-Tekinskoj ekspedicii* [Teke Ornaments with their Use for Carpets, Embroideries and other things, collected by A. Astafyev during the Akhal-Teke Expedition], Vyp. 1, s.d. (1885), p. 1 [24 dessins].

[448] G.N. Chabrov, "Pjatdesjat let nazad [Fifty years ago]", *Sredneaziatskij Universitet* [Central Asian University], 1956, n° 15-16, Nov. 6th.

[449] See note 441.

[450] The collections are at the Museum of Anthropology and Ethnography (Kunstkamera, Nr. 1325, 1790, 1802, 1928). V.A. Prishchepova, *op.cit.* (note 71), p. 79.

[451] A participant in the Akhal-Tekin expedition (1879), Astafyev collected and copied specimens of Tekin ornament (see note 447); D.M. Rezvoi and K. Dickhof made some drawings of ancient monuments and works of traditional art.

[452] G.N. Chabrov, *Pervye russkie khudozhniki v Turkestane (Pervye dva pokolenija), 1839-1890 gg.* [First Russian Artists in Turkestan (The First Two Generations) 1839-1890], a manuscript from 1948 in the Archives of the Institute of Fine Art Khamza, IZh, Ch-12, N° 93, 152 p.; S.M. Krukovskaja, *Pervye russkie khudozhniki v Srednej Azii. 1890-1900 gg.* [First Russian Artists in Central Asia], a manuscript in the Archives of the Institute of Fine Art Khamza, IZh, K-84, N° 61, 110 p.; V.G. Dolinskaja, *Khudozhniki Rossii v Srednej Azii i Kazakhstane (seredina XVIII-nachalo XX vv.) [Russian Artists in Central Asia and Kazakhstan (Mid 18th-early 20th century)]*, Moscow, 1993, 68 p.

[453] The Tretyakov Gallery, the Russian State Museum, A.S. Pushkin Museum of Fine Arts, the Museum of The Culture of Oriental Peoples, Tashkent Art Museum, the Art Museum in Nukus, etc.

[454] S. Gorshenina, B. Chukhovich, *op. cit.* (note 194); S. Gorshenina, "L'Orientalisme au Turkestan russe", in *Chemins d'étoiles. Au fil des routes de la soie*, Paris, Transboréal, 2003, p. 242-250.

[455] Thus far, only a small number of photographs show Turkestan in the period of Russian rule. See: *Au pays sacré des anciens Turcs / Eski Türklerin Kutsal Ülkesinde* [photographs by H. Bouillane de Lacoste],

Réunion des Musées nationaux /Yapï Kredi Yayïnlarï, Istanbul - Paris, 1995; E. Çagatay, *Once Upon a time in Central Asia*, Istanbul, 1996); Ch. Daney, *Le Transsibérien. Documents photographiques de la Société de géographie de Paris*, Paris, Herscher, 1980; G. Dopffer, *Paul Nadar. De la Turquie au Turkestan* [...], Istanbul, 1994; B.B. Fabritskii, I.P. Chmelev, *Khiva*, Leningrad, Aurora art Publishers, 1973; S. Gorshenina, *op.cit.* (note 235); W. Kenneth, *Frontière d'Asie. Photographies et notes de voyage du fonds Louis Martin*, Paris, Imprimerie Nationale, 1933; E. Maillart, N. Bouvier, *La vie immédiate. Photographies*, Paris, Payot, Lausanne, Ed. 24 heures, 1991; D. Girardin, *Ella Maillart sur les routes de l'Orient*, Lausanne, Actes Sud, Musée de l'Élysée, Musée Olympique, 2003; A.G. Nadvetskiy (ed.), *Boukhara (Juste a temps: les grandes archives photographiques [1871-1898])*, trad. de l'anglais par M. Suchaud, Reading, Garnet Publ.; Paris, EDIFRA, 1993; V.V. Naumkin (ed.), *Samarcande (Juste à temps: les grandes archives photographiques [1871-1898], I)*, trad. de l'anglais par S. Mendez, Reading, Garnet Publ.; Paris, EDIFRA, 1992. (English Edition: *Caught in Time: Great Photographic Archives*).

[456]See note 6. There are three specimens; one is in the Uzbekistan National Library Navoi (Tashkent), the second is at the Institute of the History of Material Culture (Saint-Petersburg; with an important collection of photographs) and the last one is in the Museum of Anthropology and Ethnography (Kunstkamera). It has been published on CD-ROM (Media Land, Tashkent, 2003).

[457]The funds of the Museum of Ethnography comprise 99 photographic collections (5,255 pictures). 15 collections belong to S.M. Dudin (over 1,500 pictures): S.P. Rusejkina, *loc.cit.* (note 99), p. 40. S.M. Dudin's other collections are at the Kunstkamera (Nr. 2123, 2124, 2636, 1199, 2413, 2450). V.A. Prishchepova, *op.cit.* (note 71), p. 74-75; A.S. Morozova, "Turkmenija v fotokollekcijakh S.M. Dudina [Turkmenistan in S.M. Dudin's photographic collections]", *Ocherki khozjajstva i kul'tury Turkmen* [Sketches of the Economy and Culture of the Turkmen], Ashkhabad, 1973.

[458]Collection housed in the Museum of Anthropology and Ethnography (Kunstkamera, Nr. 511). V.A. Prishchepova, *op.cit.* (note 71), p. 72-76.

[459]B.V. Lunin, *Istoriografija...*, *op. cit.* (note 159), p. 170-172, 199, 204, 207, 208; *Idem, Iz istorii russkogo vostokovedenija...*, *op. cit.* (note 373), p. 26, 251, 252. B.A. Golender, *Okno v proshloe: fotografija*

Russkogo Turkestana [Windows on the Past: Photographs of Russian Turkestan], Tashkent, 2002; V.A. Prishchepova, *op.cit.* (note 71), p. 72-76.

[460] Today, there are over 5,200 photographs (negatives and positives on paper and glass) in Europe in various collections: Archives Nationales de France; Bibliothèque Nationale de France, les départements des manuscrits, des cartes et plans, des estampes et de la photographie (the collection of the *Société de Geographie*); Musée du quai Branly (the collection of L. Blot); Musée-Hôtel Le Vergeur (the collection of H. Krafft, Reims, France); Maison Reveillon (the collection of L. Blot, France); Archives photographiques de Saint-Quentin-en-Yvelines (the collection of P. Nadar, France); Private Archives of the Chaffanjon Family (the collection of J. Chaffanjon, France); of Michel Vaissier (the collection of L. Gay, France); Musée d'histoire de Berne (the collection of H. Moser, Switzerland); Musée de l'Elysée de Lausanne (the collection of E. Maillart, Switzerland); *National Museum at Copenhagen* (the collection of O. Olufsen); Das Ethnographische Museum in Berlin and in Stuttgart (the collection of R.W. Rickmers); Istituto Militare di Firenze (the collection of Filippo de Filippi).

[461] S. Gorshenina, *Stanovlenie i razvitie sistemy izuchenija istorii iskusstv Srednej Azii v Uzbekistane. Konec XIX – pervaja polovina XX veka. (Istoriograficheskie aspekty)* [Birth and development of the system of studies on the history of art of Central Asia in Uzbekistan, end of 19th-mid 20th cent. (historiogaphical aspects)], Tashkent [PhD thesis], 1996.

Iconographical references*

1-4 – *Turkestanskij sbornik* (note 6), t. 527. © MediaLand, Tashkent, Uzbekistan.

5 – J.-A. Castagné, "Drevnosti Kirgizskoj stepi i Orenburgskogo kraja s risunkami Kastan'e" [Antiques of the Kirghiz Steppe and of the Orenburg's District with Castagné's drawings], *Trudy Orenburgskoj Uchenoj Arkhivnoj Komissii* [Proceedings of the Orenburg's Learned Archives Committee], XXII, 1910.

6 – © National Museum of History at Reghistan in Samarkand, Uzbekistan.

7 – M. de Ujfalvy-Bourdon, *De Paris à Samarcande* (note 122), p. 201.

8 – © Anahita Gallery, Inc, Santa Fe, New Mexico, USA.

9 – *Turkestanskij al'bom* [Turkestanian Album], t. 10: *Handicrafts*, by A.L. Kun and M.I. Brobovsky, 1871-1872, p. 42. © MediaLand, Tashkent, Uzbekistan.

10 – © Musée du Quai Branly, Paris, France.

11 – *Turkestanskij al'bom* [Turkestanian Album], t. 9: *Ethnography* (ref. fig. 9), p. 6. © MediaLand, Tashkent, Uzbekistan.

12 – H. Moser, *A travers l'Asie centrale* (note 47), opposite p. 152.

13 – A.G. Nadvetskiy (ed.), *Boukhara* (note 455), p. 93.

14 – *Turkestanskij al'bom* [Turkestan Album], t. 9: *Ethnography* (ref. fig. 9), p. 7. © MediaLand, Tashkent, Uzbekistan.

15 – *Turkestanskij al'bom* [Turkestanian Album], t. 10: *Handicrafts* (ref. fig. 9), p. 7. © MediaLand, Tashkent, Uzbekistan.

16 – *Ibidem*, p. 7. © MediaLand, Tashkent, Uzbekistan.

17 – *Ibidem*, p. 10. © MediaLand, Tashkent, Uzbekistan.

18 – *Ibidem*, p. 6. © MediaLand, Tashkent, Uzbekistan.

19 – *Ibidem*, p. 9. © MediaLand, Tashkent, Uzbekistan.

20 – © National Museum of History at Reghistan in Samarkand, Uzbekistan.

21 – *Turkestanskij al'bom* [Turkestanian Album], t. 9: *Ethnography* (ref. fig. 9), p. 5. © MediaLand, Tashkent, Uzbekistan.

22 – *Ibidem*, p. 50. © MediaLand, Tashkent, Uzbekistan.

23 – © National Museum of History at Reghistan in Samarkand, Uzbekistan.

24 – © National Museum of History at Reghistan in Samarkand, Uzbekistan.

25 – *Vsemirnaja illustracija* [Universal Illustration], n° 596. In: *Turkestanskij sbornik* (note 6), t. 287. © MediaLand, Tashkent, Uzbekistan.

---

* In spite of serious efforts, we have not been able to get explicit permits for the reproduction of all photographs, but of course the source of all illustrations has been indicated.

26 – *Turkestanskij al'bom* [Turkestanian Album], t. 10: *Handicrafts* (ref. fig. 9), p. 48. © MediaLand, Tashkent, Uzbekistan.

27 – A.G. Nadvetskiy (ed.), *Boukhara* (note 455), p. 94.

28 – *Turkestanskij al'bom* [Turkestanian Album], t. 10: *Handicrafts* (ref. fig. 9), p. 23. © MediaLand, Tashkent, Uzbekistan.

29 – © National Museum of History at Reghistan in Samarkand, Uzbekistan.

30 – © National Museum of History at Reghistan in Samarkand, Uzbekistan.

31 – P. Bernard (note 66), opposite p. 28, pl. VIII.

32 – © National Museum of History at Reghistan in Samarkand, Uzbekistan.

33 – © François Guichard, Paris, France.

34 – © J.-J. Fehr, O. Weber, Switzerland.

35 – © National Museum of History at Reghistan in Samarkand, Uzbekistan.

36 – *Turkestanskij sbornik* (note 6), t. 589: V.L. Vjatkin, *Otchet o raskopkakh observatorii Ulugbeka v 1908 I 1909 godakh* Report about the excavations of the Ulugbek's Observatory in Samarkand], p. 100. © MediaLand, Tashkent, Uzbekistan.

37 – © National Museum of History at Reghistan in Samarkand, Uzbekistan.

38 – © National Museum of History at Reghistan in Samarkand, Uzbekistan.

39 – © Ruslan Muradov, Ashkhabad.

40 – © National Museum of History at Reghistan in Samarkand, Uzbekistan.

41 – H. Moser, *A travers l'Asie centrale* (note 47), opposite p. 6.

42 – *Ibidem*, opposite p. 180.

43 – *Ibidem*, p. 284.

44 – © National Museum of History at Reghistan in Samarkand, Uzbekistan.

45 – *Atlas des étoffes, bijoux, aiguières, émaux, etc. de l'Asie centrale* (note 50, 182), pl. I.

46 – G. Pougatchenkova, A. Khakimov, *L'Art de l'Asie centrale*, Leningrad, Aurore éditions d'art, 1988, fig. 261.

47 – *Turkestanskij al'bom* [Turkestanian Album], t. 10: *Handicrafts* (ref. fig. 9), p. 19. © MediaLand, Tashkent, Uzbekistan.

48 – *Ibidem*, p. 31. © MediaLand, Tashkent, Uzbekistan.

49 – © National Museum of History at Reghistan in Samarkand, Uzbekistan.

50 – *Turkestanskij sbornik* (note 6), t. 546, p. 149. © MediaLand, Tashkent, Uzbekistan.

51 – *Turkestanskij al'bom* [Turkestanian Album], t. 7: *Archaelogy* (ref. fig. 9), p. 25. © MediaLand, Tashkent, Uzbekistan.

52 – *Turkestanskij sbornik* (note 6), t. 413: E. Boulangier, "Voyage à

Merv", *Le tour du Monde*, 1887, LIII, p. 21. © MediaLand, Tashkent, Uzbekistan.

53 – *Atlas des étoffes, bijoux, aiguières, émaux, etc. de l'Asie centrale* (note 50, 182), pl. VI.

54 – *Atlas des étoffes, bijoux, aiguières, émaux, etc. de l'Asie centrale* (note 50, 182), pl. XIV.

55 – R.N. Balsiger, E.J. Kläy, *Bei Schah, Emir und Khan.* (note 148), p. 192.

56 – *Ibidem*, p. 200.

57 – CGA RUz, F. P-2773, cat. 1, f. 164.

58 – *Idem*.

59 – © Société de géographie, Paris.

60 – *Album of the Turkestan Exhibition of Agricultural and Industrial Objects in 1886 at Tashkent.* National Library Navoy, Tashkent. Repr. from B.V. Lunin (note 120), p. 34.

61 – *Turkestanskij sbornik* (note 6), t. 34: Supplement of Vsemirnaja Illustracija, n° 86, p. 1. © MediaLand, Tashkent, Uzbekistan.

62 – *Turkestanskij sbornik* (note 6), t. 42, p. 84. © MediaLand, Tashkent, Uzbekistan.

63 – *Ibidem*, p. 85. © MediaLand, Tashkent, Uzbekistan.

64 – *Protokoly Turkestanskogo kruzhka ljubitelej arkheologii*, XIII, Tashkent, 1909, pl. I.

65 – *Turkestanskij sbornik* (note 6), t. 578, p. 3. © MediaLand, Tashkent, Uzbekistan.

66 – *Turkestanskij sbornik* (note 6, 18), t. 262, p. 308. © MediaLand, Tashkent, Uzbekistan.

67 – A.G. Nadvetskiy (ed.), *Boukhara* (note 455), p. 49.

68 – *Turkestanskij sbornik* (note 6), t. 287, p. 17. © MediaLand, Tashkent, Uzbekistan.

69– © The Michel Vaissier's collection.

70 – H. Moser, *A travers l'Asie centrale* (note 47), opposite p. of title.

71 – *Ibidem*, opposite p. 248.

72 – *Ibidem*, p. 312.

73 – *Turkestanskij sbornik* (note 6). © MediaLand, Tashkent, Uzbekistan.

74 – H. Moser, *A travers l'Asie centrale* (note 47), p. 187.

75 – *Atlas des étoffes, bijoux, aiguières, émaux, etc. de l'Asie centrale* (note 50, 182), pl. XIII.

76 – *Ibidem*, pl. XVIII.

77 – H. Moser, *A travers l'Asie centrale* (note 47), opposite p. 72.

78 – *Ibidem*, opposite p. 157.

79 – *Ibidem*, p. 264.

80 – © National Museum of History at Reghistan in Samarkand, Uzbekistan.

81 – H. *Moser, A travers l'Asie centrale* (note 47), p. 24.

82 – Moshkova (note 53), next to plate LIV.

83 – *Atlas des étoffes, bijoux, aiguières, émaux, etc. de l'Asie centrale* (note 50, 182), pl. XVI.

84 – Henri Moser, © Bernisches Historisches Museum.

85 – V.I. Masalskij, *Turkestanskij Kraj*, Sankt-Peterburg, 1913, p. 533.

86 – A.G. Nadvetskiy (ed.), *Boukhara* (note 455), p. 100.

87 – *Ibidem*, p. 99.

88 – *Turkestanskij al'bom* [Turkestanian Album], t. 9 : *Ethnography* (ref. fig. 9), p. 6. © MediaLand, Tashkent, Uzbekistan.

89 – *Turkestanskij al'bom* [Turkestanian Album], t. 1 : *History* (ref. fig. 9), p. 18. © MediaLand, Tashkent, Uzbekistan.

90 – © National Museum of History at Reghistan in Samarkand, Uzbekistan.

91 – © National Museum of History at Reghistan in Samarkand, Uzbekistan.

92 – *Album of the Turkestan Exhibition of Agricultural and Industrial Objects in 1886 at Tashkent. National Library Navoy,* Tashkent. Repr. from B.V. Lunin (note 120), p. 33.

93 – *Turkestanskij sbornik* (note 6), t. 374 : A.V. Komarov, *Russkie v Afganistane* [Russians at Afghanistan], Saint-Petersburg, 1885, p. 1. © MediaLand, Tashkent, Uzbekistan.

94 – *Protokoly Turkestanskogo kruzhka ljubitelej arkheologii*, XIII, Tashkent, 1909, plate.

95 – © National Museum of History at Reghistan in Samarkand, Uzbekistan.

96 – © National Museum of History at Reghistan in Samarkand, Uzbekistan.

97 – © National Museum of History at Reghistan in Samarkand, Uzbekistan.

98 – Ref. fig. 5, Pl. XI.

99 – *Turkestanskij sbornik* (note 6), t. 287, p. 9. © MediaLand, Tashkent, Uzbekistan.

100 – © National Museum of History at Reghistan in Samarkand, Uzbekistan.

101 – *Atlas des étoffes, bijoux, aiguières, émaux, etc. de l'Asie centrale* (note 50, 182), pl. XXIV.

102 – *Ibidem*, pl. XX.

103 – *Turkestanskij al'bom* [Turkestanian Album], t. 8 : *Ethnography* (ref. fig. 9), p. 3. © MediaLand, Tashkent, Uzbekistan.

104 – H. Moser, *A travers l'Asie centrale* (note 47), opposite p. 184.

105 – © National Museum of History at Reghistan in Samarkand, Uzbekistan.

106 – N. Veselovsky, *Descriptions des mosquées de Samarcande, 1895-1899.*

107 – *Ibidem*.

Index

Addenda:

Note 8: For examples of publications on the contemporary collections see: K. Fitz Gibbon, A. Hale, *Ikat Silks of Central Asia: the Guido Goldman Collection,* London: L. King, A. Marcuson, 1997; E.J. Grub, *Keshte. Central Asian Embroideries. The Marshall and Marilyn R. Wolf Collection*, London, Robert Marcuson Publishing Service, 2003.

Note 68: See also: S. Hodjash, "Ancient Egyptian objects discovered on the territory of the USSR", *Sesto Congresso internazionale di egittologia, Atti I*, Torino, 1992, p. 265-272; *eadem, Ancient Egyptian Scarabs. A Catalogue of Seals and Scarabs from Museums in Russia, Ukraine, the Caucasus and the Baltic States*, Moscow, 1999.

Note 88: A. Banck, *The Oriental Collections at the Hermitage Museum (General charasteristic and main trends of investigation)* (XXVth International Congress of Orientalists), Leningrad, The State Hermitage Edition, 1960, p. 6 (in Russian).

Note 126: A. Banck, *ibidem*, p. 7.

Note 396: A. Banck, *ibidem*, p. 7.